Canadian Daily Language Activities

— Grade 3 —

Written by Eleanor M. Summers

Our Canadian Daily Language Activities series provides short and quick opportunities for students to review and reinforce skills in punctuation, grammar, spelling, language and reading comprehension. The Bonus Activities that follow each week of skills are fun tasks such as word and vocabulary puzzles, figurative language and reading exercises. A short interesting fact about Canada is the finishing touch!

ELEANOR M. SUMMERS is a retired teacher who is still actively involved in education. She has created many resources in language, science and history. As a writer, she enjoys creating practical and thought-provoking resources for teachers and parents.

Published in Canada by:
On The Mark Press
15 Dairy Avenue, Napanee, Ontario, K7R 1M4
www.onthemarkpress.com

Funded by the
Government
of Canada

SSR1146   ISBN: 9781771587327 © On The Mark Press

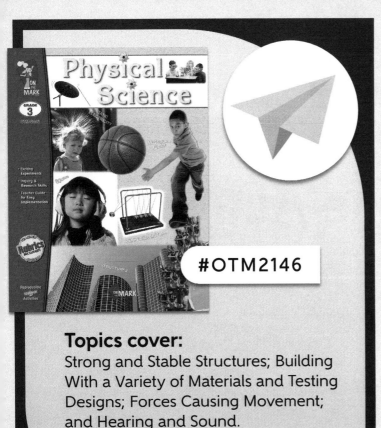

#OTM2146

Topics cover:
Strong and Stable Structures; Building With a Variety of Materials and Testing Designs; Forces Causing Movement; and Hearing and Sound.

#OTM2154

Topics cover:
Exploring Soils in the Environment, Rocks and Minerals and Stars and Planets.

Each resource has been developed to cover the overall expectations of the Social Studies Curriculum. These units can be used as a whole to fulfill the overall expectation requirements or it can be used by activity to compliment other resources and activities. Includes Lesson Plans, Extension Activities, Teacher Guide and Assessments.

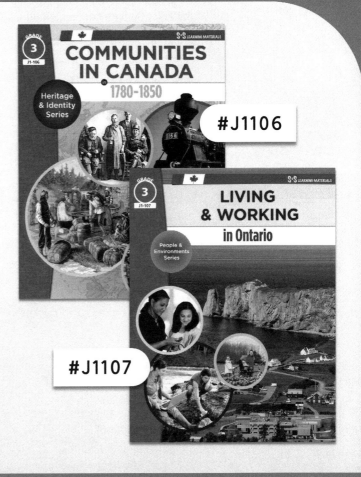

#J1106

#J1107

HOW TO USE: CANADIAN DAILY LANGUAGE ACTIVITIES

This book is divided into 32 weekly sections.

Each weekly section provides daily skill review and assessment activities.

ACTIVITIES 1 – 4

Focus is on:

- punctuation, capitalization, grammar, and spelling
- language and reading comprehension skills

ACTIVITY 5

Focus is on:

- a single language or reading skill

BONUS ACTIVITY

Provides opportunities for extended activities.

- word puzzles, vocabulary development
- spelling
- reading skills
- includes a short, interesting fact about Canada

STUDENT PROGRESS CHART

- Students record their daily score for each Language Activity.
- At the end of the week, they calculate their Total Score
- At the end of four weeks, students evaluate their performance.
- Students will require one copy of page 3 and three copies of page 4 to record results for entire 32 weeks. Teachers may wish to make back-to-back copies.

TEACHER SUGGESTIONS

- All activities may be completed for each week or teachers may exclude some.
- New skills may be completed as a whole class activity.
- Bonus Activities may be used at teachers' discretion.
- Correcting student work together will help model the correct responses.
- Monitor student mastery of skills from information on the Student Progress Chart.

_____ 'S PROGRESS CHART

How many did you get correct each day? Record your score on the chart.

Week	Activity 1	Activity 2	Activity 3	Activity 4	Activity 5	Total Score
#	/5	/5	/5	/5	/5	/25

Week	Activity 1	Activity 2	Activity 3	Activity 4	Activity 5	Total Score
#	/5	/5	/5	/5	/5	/25

Week	Activity 1	Activity 2	Activity 3	Activity 4	Activity 5	Total Score
#	/5	/5	/5	/5	/5	/25

Week	Activity 1	Activity 2	Activity 3	Activity 4	Activity 5	Total Score
#	/5	/5	/5	/5	/5	/25

My strongest skills are _____

My skills that need improvement are _____

The Bonus Activities I liked best are _____

Week	Activity 1	Activity 2	Activity 3	Activity 4	Activity 5	Total Score
#	/5	/5	/5	/5	/5	/25

Week	Activity 1	Activity 2	Activity 3	Activity 4	Activity 5	Total Score
#	/5	/5	/5	/5	/5	/25

Week	Activity 1	Activity 2	Activity 3	Activity 4	Activity 5	Total Score
#	/5	/5	/5	/5	/5	/25

Week	Activity 1	Activity 2	Activity 3	Activity 4	Activity 5	Total Score
#	/5	/5	/5	/5	/5	/25

My strongest skills are _____

My skills that need improvement are _____

The Bonus Activities I liked best are _____

SSR1146   ISBN: 9781771587327 © On The Mark Press

_____ 'S PROGRESS CHART

How many did you get correct each day? Record your score on the chart.

Week	Activity 1	Activity 2	Activity 3	Activity 4	Activity 5	Total Score
#	/5	/5	/5	/5	/5	/25

Week	Activity 1	Activity 2	Activity 3	Activity 4	Activity 5	Total Score
#	/5	/5	/5	/5	/5	/25

Week	Activity 1	Activity 2	Activity 3	Activity 4	Activity 5	Total Score
#	/5	/5	/5	/5	/5	/25

Week	Activity 1	Activity 2	Activity 3	Activity 4	Activity 5	Total Score
#	/5	/5	/5	/5	/5	/25

My strongest skills are _____

My skills that need improvement are _____

The Bonus Activities I liked best are _____

Week	Activity 1	Activity 2	Activity 3	Activity 4	Activity 5	Total Score
#	/5	/5	/5	/5	/5	/25

Week	Activity 1	Activity 2	Activity 3	Activity 4	Activity 5	Total Score
#	/5	/5	/5	/5	/5	/25

Week	Activity 1	Activity 2	Activity 3	Activity 4	Activity 5	Total Score
#	/5	/5	/5	/5	/5	/25

Week	Activity 1	Activity 2	Activity 3	Activity 4	Activity 5	Total Score
#	/5	/5	/5	/5	/5	/25

My strongest skills are _____

My skills that need improvement are _____

The Bonus Activities I liked best are _____

SSR1146   ISBN: 9781771587327 © On The Mark Press

DAILY LANGUAGE ACTIVITIES SKILLS LIST

This book provides many opportunities for practice of the following skills:

VOCABULARY & WORD SKILLS

- word meaning from context
- root words/prefixes/suffixes
- vowel sounds
- spelling
- syllabication
- synonyms/antonyms/homonyms
- contractions
- rhyming

CAPITALIZATION

- beginning of sentences
- proper names/titles of people
- names of places
- titles of books, songs, poems
- names of days, months, holidays
- abbreviations

PUNCTUATION

- punctuation at the end of a sentence
- commas in a series
- commas in dates and addresses
- commas in simple dialogue
- periods in abbreviations
- use of the colon in time
- quotation marks in speech
- quotation marks: poems, songs, stories
- apostrophes in contractions
- apostrophes in possessives
- punctuation in a friendly letter
- run on sentences
- underlining: books, plays, poems, magazines

GRAMMAR & WORD USAGE

- pronouns
- common/proper nouns
- singular/plural nouns
- possessive nouns
- verb forms
- double negatives
- adjectives
- correct article/determiner
- adverbs
- parts of speech
- comparative/superlative
- subject/predicate
- subject – verb agreement
- identifying sentences
- sentence types
- sentence combinations

READING COMPREHENSION

- analogies
- categorization
- cause and effect
- fact or opinion
- fact or fiction / fantasy
- fiction or nonfiction
- figurative language
- inference

REFERENCE SKILLS

- alphabetical order
- dictionary skills
- reference materials

SSR1146   ISBN: 9781771587327 © On The Mark Press

Name: _____

Correct these sentences.

1. does you like kittens or puppies best

_____

2. me and my sister like to help our mom

_____

Circle the word that is spelled correctly.

3.   abel   abul   able   ayble

4.   gost   ghoste   ghoast   ghost

Write two words that rhyme with this word.

5. near _____   _____

Name: _____

Sentence **or** *not a sentence*?

1. Our new Prime Minister.   _____

2. We sing our national anthem each day.   _____

Correct these sentences.

3. a good book to reed is the incredible journey

_____

4. mrs davis, our neighbour, bakes the bestest cookies

_____

Common **or** *proper noun?*

5. Toronto Maple Leafs   _____

Name: _____

Use context clues to explain the meaning of the underlined word.

1. We stood in <u>awe</u> watching Niagara Falls _____

Correct these sentences.

2. has you ever traveled on a boat on lake ontario

_____

3. jake wants too go to toronto metro zoo

_____

Circle the correct way to divide each word into syllables.

4. wi – nter   win – ter   wint – er   winte – r

5. fidd – le   fi – ddle   fid – dle   fiddl – e

Name: _____

Write the number of syllables you hear in each word.

1. elevator   _____

2. mountainous   _____

Correct these sentences.

3. we is going to pizza palace for ella's birthday

_____

4. i am buying her a great book called ramona

_____

Circle the correct abbreviation for "Friday".

5. Frid.   Fridy.   Fri.   Fr.

      SSR1146   ISBN: 9781771587327 © On The Mark Press

Name: _____

What reference source would be best to find information for these things? Write *encyclopedia*, *dictionary*, *cookbook*, or *telephone book*.

1. the correct spelling of "kilometre"   _____

2. a recipe for apple spice cookies   _____

3. the phone number for Harry's Hamburgers _____

4. the history of the game of hockey   _____

5. how to pronounce the word " ketchup"   _____

Name: _____

Bonus Activity: Names that Need Capitals

Words that name specific people or places need capital letters.

Match the words in the box with the words that describe them.

1. a weekday   _____

2. a street   _____

3. our country   _____

4. July 1   _____

5. Canada's capital   _____

6. a month   _____

| Canada Day |
| Ottawa |
| Main Street |
| Canada |
| June |
| Friday |

MY CANADA

The Rideau Canal, is the oldest operating canal system in North America.
It runs from the Ottawa River to Lake Ontario and the St. Lawrence River at Kingston.

Name: _____

Correct these sentences.

1.   the movie we want to watch is on tv at 730 on tuesday

_____

2.   is your favourite holiday easter or thanksgiving

_____

Write the two words that make up each contraction.

3.   don't   _____

4.   they'll   _____

Synonym or *antonym*?

5.   cash, money   _____

- -

Name: _____

Write the *root* or *base* word for each word.

1.   carelessness   _____

2.   daily   _____

Fact or *fiction*?

3.   The Great Lakes are in Manitoba.   _____

Correct these sentences.

4.   i used an atlas to locate the gaspe said mike

_____

5.   our family is going there in july he added

_____

SSR1146   ISBN: 9781771587327 © On The Mark Press

Name: _____

What do these words have in common?

1.   loonie , quarter, nickle, toonie   _____

Correct these sentences.

2.   my sister leah is two small to go down this slide

_____

3.   what were the final score of the basketball game

_____

Complete these analogies.

4.   Dog is to bark as cow is to _____

5.   Glove is to hand as shoe is to _____

Name: _____

Correct these sentences.

1.   will you cheer for the oilers or the flames in saturday's game

_____

2.   my cousins both go to briar hill middle school said jenny

_____

Use context clues to explain the meaning of the underlined word.

3.   "It is your <u>responsibility</u> to look after your belongings," said Mom.

_____

Write a *common noun* for each proper noun.

4.   Montreal Canadiens   _____

5.   Patrick Chan   _____

Name: _____

When words are in a certain order, we say they are *in sequence*. Complete each sequence by filling in the word that comes next.

1. Monday, Tuesday, Wednesday _____

2. spring summer, autumn _____

3. five, ten, fifteen _____

4. day, week, month, _____

5. first, second, third, _____

- -

Name: _____

Bonus Activity: Tell a Story

Number each sentence in the correct order. Illustrate each sentence.

___ She waved her hand high in the air.	
___ Kelly stumbled and fell into the deep snowbank.	
___ Heather saw her waving and came to help her friend.	
___ The girls laughed when the "rescue" was complete.	

BONUS ACTIVIT

The Holstein is the most common cow breed in Canada (94% of the country's cows). Glass of milk, anyone?

MY CANADA

SSR1146   ISBN: 9781771587327 © On The Mark Press

Correct these sentences.

1.   him and i play on the same soccer team, the tigers

_____

2.   my sister, susan, are getting married on august 21 2016

_____

Singular or *plural*?

3.   babies   _____

4.   dress   _____

Circle the words that have the same sound as the "o" in "no".

5.   though   come   ghost   gold   log   on

- -

Sentence or not a sentence?

1.   The moose is a huge animal.   _____

2.   Snow on the roads.   _____

Correct these sentences.

3.   are the rocky mountains in british columbia asked pete

_____

4.   we loves the easter egg hunt at aunt may's each year

_____

Circle the adjectives in this sentence.

5.   The   beautiful   flowers   are   red,   yellow   and   orange.

What do these words have in common?

1. raccoon, beaver, porcupine, skunk _____

2. hockey, figure skating, snowshoeing, skiing _____

Correct these sentences.

3. the great gilly hopkins is a good story said ms blake

_____

4. we have a copy in our school library added freddie

_____

Synonym or antonym?

5. fail, succeed _____

Tell if the underlined word is a *noun* or a *verb*.

1. Our <u>bus</u> got stuck in the snow. _____

2. The tow truck <u>pulled</u> us out. _____

Correct these sentences.

3. jack said we ain't never been hiking down that trail

_____

4. bring that there compass or we will get losted suggested gerry

_____

Write a good sentence for this pair of homonyms.

5. sale, sail _____

SSR1146   ISBN: 9781771587327 © On The Mark Press

Name: _____

Read the following sentences. Decide if the underlined part has a *capitalization* error, a *punctuation* error, a *spelling* error or *no mistake*.

1. <u>last</u> night I dreamed I was ten centimetres tall. _____

2. I could walk right under my bed <u>without hitting my head</u>.

   _____

3. Lucky for me my mom wasn't in my <u>dreem</u>. _____

4. What would she say about all the stuff under <u>my bed</u>

   _____

5. <u>What a relief</u> The next morning everything was normal.

   _____

Name: _____

Bonus Activity: Fact or Opinion

Read the following sentences. Decide if they are a fact or an opinion. Write *Fact* or *Opinion* on the line.

1. Soccer is the best sport in the world! _____

2. Her grandmother lives in Moose Jaw, Saskatchewan. _____

3. My mother makes the best chocolate cake. _____

4. We have five new computers in our computer lab. _____

5. You will never walk all the way to the top of that hill. _____

MY CANADA

Baseball legend, Babe Ruth, hit his first professional home run in Toronto on Sept. 5, 1914.

Name: _____

Correct these sentences.

1. where is we goin on our class trip asked ricky

_____

2. how about the royal ontario museum suggested mr cumings

_____

Common or *proper* noun?

3. Halifax _____

Circle the words that have two syllables.

4.   hockey   basketball   baseball   badminton

5.   Kingston   Montreal   Vancouver   Brandon

WEEK
4

ACTIVIT
1

TOTAL
/5

Name: _____

Write a good sentence for this pair of homophones: eye, I

1. _____ .

Write the plural form of each noun.

2. shelf _____

3. woman _____

Correct these sentences.

4. sarah and becky brung juice boxes too the class party

_____

5. lets join that there game of soccer with them there boys

_____

WEEK
4

ACTIVIT
2

TOTAL
/5

SSR1146   ISBN: 9781771587327 © On The Mark Press

Name: _____

Where does each event likely take place?

1. I sat down and fastened my seat belt quickly. _____

2. He shoots! He scores! _____

Correct these sentences.

3. pollys favorit plase to eat is golden grill on main street

_____

4. them serves the best bergers and frys in the hole town

_____

Circle the word that does not belong.

5. caribou   moose   zebra   elk   reindeer

- -

Name: _____

Divide each word into syllables.

1. wolverine _____

2. Edmonton _____

Correct these sentences.

3. a totem are an animal or object that is a symbol of a famly or tribe

_____

4. when the symbols is carved on logs, they make a totem pol

_____

Circle the correct abbreviation for "doctor"

5. dr.   Doc.   Dr.   Dtr.   Dcr.

Combine the two sentences to make one good sentence.

1. The wind howled. The snow blew into high drifts.

_____

2. The water is cold. The sun is warm.

_____

3. My friend is coming over. We are going to see a movie.

_____

4. Our team won the trophy. Our picture was in the newspaper.

_____

5. My brother's alarm is noisy. It wakes me up every day.

_____

Name: _____

Bonus Activity: Adjectives

Adjectives describe people, places or things. **Solve the puzzle by filling in the correct adjective.**

BONUS
ACTIVIT

	Clue						
1	A very small creature is						
2	A simple problem is						
3	A Canadian soldier is						
4	A person who is easily frightened is						
5	A jolly person is						
6	An intelligent person is						

Singer-songwriter Bryan Adams was the first Canadian musician to sell one million albums for his 1984 album Reckless. This star was born in Kingston, Ontario.

MY CANADA

SSR1146   ISBN: 9781771587327 © On The Mark Press

Name: _____

Singular or *plural*?

1.   cookies   _____

Correct these sentences.

2.   carol asked who spilled my milk all over my desk

_____

3.   laura, carols frend, had saw who made the miss

_____

Write *statement*, *command*, *question* or *exclamation* to tell the kind of sentence.

4.   What time is it?   _____

5.   I will give you a ride to school.   _____

Name: _____

Fact or *fantasy*?

1.   Cinderella is a fairy tale and a movie.   _____

2.   A pumpkin changes into a golden coach.   _____

Correct these sentences.

3.   give me your phone number me will call you tonight

_____

4.   harry and sam is werking on that there project to gether

_____

Give your opinion of the following topic.

5.   going to summer camp _____

_____

Write the *comparative* and *superlative* adjectives for these words.

1. good   _____   _____

2. sunny   _____   _____

Underline the *cause* and circle the *effect* in this sentence.

3. We stayed indoors for recess because it was raining hard outside.

Correct these sentences.

4. if i gives you ten dimes, will you gives me a loonie

    _____

5. they're were a gold ring setting on the window sill by the sank

    _____

Circle the singular nouns.

1.   tree   branches   apple   leaves   twig

Correct these sentences.

2. how much muney does you have in your pockit

    _____

3. don't leave you bike in the driveway said my dad

    _____

Complete the analogies.

4. moon is to night as sun is to _____

5. whale is to huge as ant is to _____

SSR1146   ISBN: 9781771587327 © On The Mark Press

Name: _____

Write the word on the line that best completes each sentence.

1. We are _____ (**goes / going**) to Sudbury to visit our grandparents.

2. We need to _____ (**buy / buys**) a ticket to go on the train.

3. The person at the service desk _____ (**sold / sells**) us the right ticket.

4. We were _____ (**waited / waiting**) to get on our train.

5. Our parents _____ (**waving / waved**) goodbye to us from the platform.

Name: _____

Bonus Activity: Holiday Eating

Read the following newspaper ad for this restaurant. Complete each sentence.

———— MOM'S HOME COOKING RESTAURANT ————

Special Thanksgiving Menu

Roast Turkey Dinner	$10.50
Baked Ham Dinner	$12.00
Seafood Special	$15.00

613 – 555 – 1462

Open 10:00 am to 8:00 pm on Sunday and Monday.

1. This restaurant is advertising for the holiday of _____

2. The most expensive meal is _____

3. The restaurant is open for _____ hours on Sunday and Monday.

Montreal's Marcellus Gilmore Edson was the first person to patent

MY CANADA

modern day peanut butter.

Name: _____

Correct these sentences.

1.   this summer we is going to kids camp on whitefish lake

_____

2.   every one will bee able to go canoeing, swiming, fishing and hikeing

_____

Give the plural of each noun.

3.   potato   _____

4.   daisy   _____

Use context clues to explain the meaning of the underlined word.

5.   The helicopter <u>hovered</u> above the water.

_____

Name: _____

Write three words that rhyme with "glue".

1.   _____   _____   _____

What is this person probably doing?

2.   Mom sorted the clothes and put them into the machine.

_____

3.   Dan let out more string so it could fly higher. _____

Correct these sentences.

4.   you will needs to lisen so you will no how too do your work

_____

5.   did ned sprain his ankle in the football game asked victor

_____

SSR1146   ISBN: 9781771587327 © On The Mark Press

Name: _____

Use context clues to explain the meaning of the underlined word.

1. To be a <u>lumberjack</u> you need to be strong and a good climber.

_____

Circle the *verb* in each sentence.

2. The old truck chugged along the dusty road.

3. The rabbit nibbled at the carrots and the lettuce.

Correct these sentences.

4. has you read the pome indian summer asked miss thatcher

_____

5. we will study pionear life this here year said mr collins

_____

- -

Name: _____

Correct these sentences.

1. the magician's tricks were the best i ever seed

_____

2. he asked peeple from the audience to help hims with some tricks

_____

***Sentence* or *not a sentence*?**

3. Smelled good to eat. _____

4. Mother was cooking chicken for dinner. _____

Write one sentence using this pair of antonyms: gentle, rough

5. _____

Name: _____

Write the word that best completes each sentence.

1   _____ Mom plan to take us shopping for new shoes?

   Is / Do / Does

2.   I will help _____ with her homework if she asks me.

   she / they / her

3.   The _____ part of this movie is coming right up.

   good / better / best

4.   Here _____ Willy now. He was almost late.

   comed / come / comes

5.   Grandpa _____ building a surprise in his workshop.

   was / be / were

Name: _____

Bonus Activity: Analogies

An *analogy* is a way of comparing things to show how they are alike.
Complete these analogies.

1. Pencil is to write as brush is to _____

2. Cow is to milk as chicken is to _____

3. Crayons are to colour as scissors are to _____

4. Skating is to winter as swimming is to _____

5. Cat is to kitten as dog is to _____

6. Foot is to leg as hand is to _____

MY CANADA

George Klein, of Hamilton, Ontario, invented the electric wheelchair in 1955.

It was first used for disabled military people.

SSR1146   ISBN: 9781771587327 © On The Mark Press

Name: _____

Correct these sentences.

1. it was time for the bus to come i got my jacket

_____

2. the leafs terned red yellow and orange

_____

Circle the *adjectives* in each sentence.

3. Their new puppy has short, fluffy brown fur.

4. Ice cream is a sweet and cold treat.

***Fact* or *opinion*?**

5. All Canadians love winter!   _____

Name: _____

Write the *plural form* for the following nouns.

1. man   _____

2. baby   _____

Use these antonyms in one good sentence: damp, dry

3. _____

Correct these sentences.

4. farmer brown have cows horses and pigs on hims farm

_____

5. we studied how to spell the names of canada's provinces

_____

Name: _____

Write a synonym for:

1.   intelligent   _____

Correct these sentences.

2.   me and my sister sold our old toys at our yard sale

_____

3.   there are ice and snow at the top of that mountain

_____

Where would these events probably take place?

4.   The marching band came ahead of the clowns doing tricks.

      _____

5.   I am going to renew this book and also look for a new one. _____

Name: _____

Correct these sentences.

1.   what would you like for lunch asked mom

_____

2.   how about chicken noodle soup i answered

_____

Circle the words that have two syllables.

3.   lunch   breakfast   dinner   snack   supper

Write the possessive form of the noun.

4.   the wagon of my brother   _____

5.   the red hat belonging to Sally   _____

SSR1146   ISBN: 9781771587327 © On The Mark Press

Name: _____

What reference source would be best to find information for these things?
Write *encyclopedia*, *dictionary*, *thesaurus*, *cookbook*, or *telephone book*.

1. how to pronounce the word "pizza" _____

2. a recipe for spaghetti sauce _____

3. the area code for the city of Toronto _____

4. the name of the inventor of basketball _____

5. a synonym for the word "scurry" _____

Name: _____

Bonus Activity: Which Word Doesn't Belong?

Put an *X* on the word that doesn't belong.

1.	beak	sky	feather	claw
2.	rock	pebble	stone	moss
3.	late	happy	never	before
4.	ever	over	under	near
5.	rain	lightning	flood	water
6.	brown	tree	plant	bush

MY CANADA

The first Canadian stamp, the Three-Pence Beaver was issued on April 23, 1851.

Name: _____

Correct these sentences.

1.   many totem poles can be sean in british columbia

_____

2.   we goed there on our summer vacation last july

_____

Write the two words that make up each contraction.

3.   doesn't   _____

4.   I'm   _____

Common or proper noun?

5.   Canada's Wonderland   _____

- -

Name: _____

Complete the analogy.

1.   eye is to look as ear is to _____

2.   chair is to sit as bed is to _____

Circle the word that is spelled correctly.

3.   libary   liberary   library   libarary

Correct these sentences.

4.   its your turn to help with dishes tonite anna

_____

5.   i thinks your flashlight are brighter then mine

_____

SSR1146   ISBN: 9781771587327 © On The Mark Press

Name: _____

Write a common noun for each proper noun.

1. Winnipeg _____

2. Edmonton Oilers _____

Correct these sentences.

3. can you sing o canada in english and french

_____

4. my favourite tv show, kids speak out, is on each thursday

_____

Is this sentence a statement, interrogative, command or exclamatory?

5. Are you coming to the game with us? _____

Name: _____

Correct these sentences.

1. we was cheering and clapping for the home team

_____

2. what street do you live on asked jerry's mom

_____

Write the word that best completes the sentence.

3. _____ the best game I have ever played!

   Thats / Thats' / That's

Number these words in alphabetical order.

4. _____lightning   _____lace   _____lodge

5. _____desert   _____detail   _____devil

Name: _____

Combine these sentences to make one good sentence.

1.   Jessie is the fastest runner. He easily won the race.

_____

2.   Those cookies are hot. Mom just took them out of the oven.

_____

3.   Hector was late getting to the bus stop. He missed the bus to school.

_____

4.   We can play in my treehouse. Come to my house on Saturday.

_____

5.   Our class is going on a trip. We are going to the planetarium.

_____

Name: _____

Bonus Activity: Suffix Word Search

The box words each have a suffix. Find and circle each word in the puzzle:

t	f	n	t	u	e	j	i	s	b
t	h	e	n	d	l	e	s	s	a
b	e	a	u	t	i	f	u	l	b
w	l	t	n	o	e	a	s	t	y
w	p	l	o	k	m	p	a	m	l
s	f	y	l	e	f	a	s	i	t
m	u	t	k	o	a	u	i	b	f
y	l	o	u	d	l	y	l	h	o
c	a	r	e	f	u	l	b	k	s
i	s	s	e	l	e	c	i	r	p

thankful   helpful

beautiful   neatly

endless   loudly

softly   careful

priceless   safely

MY CANADA   *The largest log cabin in the world* is in Montebello, Quebec.
Now called the Fairmont Chateau Montebello, it has 211 rooms!

   SSR1146   ISBN: 9781771587327 © On The Mark Press

Name: _____

Present, past or *future?*

1.　The stone I threw skipped over the water.　_____

2.　I'm going to Liza's birthday party tomorrow.　_____

Correct these sentences.

3.　the bear caught a fish in its paw it ate it

_____

4.　what is our math homework for tonight asked peter

_____

Circle the word that is spelled correctly.

5.　shugar　　shuger　　sugar　　shughar

Name: _____

Add a prefix to each word.

1.　read　_____

2.　like　_____

Fact or *fiction?*

3.　Avalanches are a hazard in the Rocky Mountains.　_____

Correct these sentences.

4.　i has a cat named ginger and a fish named goldie

_____

5.　rory want to play on our school soccer teem next year

_____

Name: _____

What part of the friendly letter is this?

1. Dear Paulo _____

Correct these sentences.

2. moms job is at the queenston general hospital in surrey

_____

3. we saw a double reinbow in the sky yesterday

_____

How many syllables does each word have?

4. restaurant _____

5. Saskatchewan _____

Name: _____

Correct these sentences.

1. willy and me read a good story called the treasure of hidden bay

_____

2. it were an adventure story about too friends looking for a lost chest

_____

Use context clues to explain the meaning of the underlined word.

3. Eat your meat and vegetables first. Then you may have dessert.

_____

Where would each event probably take place?

4. "Listen carefully as I say each word," said Ms Drake. _____

5. "Try to blow out all the candles at once," said Fanny. _____

SSR1146   ISBN: 9781771587327 © On The Mark Press

Read the following sentences. Decide if the underlined part has a capitalization error, a punctuation error, a spelling error or no mistake.

1. <u>our</u> class wanted to put on a puppet show. _____

2. Our teacher, Mrs. Dunbar, <u>helped us to get started.</u> _____

3. We decided to use <u>shado</u> puppets. _____

4. <u>everyone</u> helped to write the story. _____

5. Our show was a <u>huge success</u> _____

- -

Name: _____

WEEK
9

Bonus Activity: Terrific Titles!

A good title is important for any story, book, TV show, or movie. Titles should be short and interesting. **Write a good title for each of these things:**

1. a cookbook for making foods for kids' lunches _____

2. a TV show about living in Canada's North. _____

3. a movie about being lost overnight in a thick forest

   _____

4. a book telling how to be a successful birdwatcher

   _____

5. a book about the life story of a sports hero _____

The Royal Canadian Mint made the world's first $1 million coin in 2007.

MY CANADA

The Mint sold five of the huge coins!

Name: _____

Circle the word that is spelled correctly.

1.   hurd   heared   hered   heard

2.   anser   answere   answer   ansar

Correct these sentences.

3.   i set my alarm clock for 600 am early for me

_____

4.   grandma asked will you help me weed the garden

_____

Complete the analogy.

5.   Father is to man as mother is to _____

Name: _____

Add a prefix and a suffix to each word.

1.   <u>print</u>   _____   _____

2.   appear   _____   _____

***Fact* or *opinion*?**

3.   Chocolate chip cookies are the best!   _____

Correct these sentences.

4.   i likes reading misstery stories about life on the see

_____

5.   my favorit book is monsters of the deep by j j dunn

_____

SSR1146   ISBN: 9781771587327 © On The Mark Press

Name: _____

Number these words in alphabetical order.

1. _____ neon   _____ nasty   _____ nimble   _____ napkin

Correct these sentences.

2. my vary best friends is ginny kara and adele

_____

3. them big boys was teasing the little boys on the playground

_____

Write the comparative and superlative forms of these adjectives.

4. tiny   _____   _____

5. beautiful   _____   _____

Name: _____

Correct these sentences.

1. we had maple syrup cotten candy at gibbons family farm

_____

2. will your buziness trip last long i asked dad

_____

Write two words that rhyme with this word:

3. please   _____   _____

How many syllables in each word?

4. Kelowna   _____

5. Edmundston   _____

Name: _____

Combine these sentences into one good sentence.

1. The pitcher threw the ball. I hit it. I got a home run!

   _____

2. Daffodils are pretty flowers. They grow in the spring. They are yellow.

   _____

3. Our new puppy chews everything. It chewed my new shoes. Mom was mad.

   _____

4. I have a bad cold. I need to stay in bed. I will miss school.

   _____

5. My aunt is visiting. She lives in Calgary. She will be here for two weeks.

   _____

- -

Name: _____

Bonus Activity: Same or Opposite?

Read the pairs of words.

If the words are *antonyms* (opposites), colour the box *yellow*.

If the words are *synonyms* (same), colour the box *orange*.

happy sad	note letter	speedy quick	beautiful ugly
smart clever	rabbit bunny	often never	chair seat
strong weak	icy hot	carpet rug	new used

MY CANADA

Laura Secord, founded in 1913, is Canada's largest seller of chocolate.

SSR1146   ISBN: 9781771587327 © On The Mark Press

Correct these sentences.

1. my dentist, dr forrester, told me to brush my tooths more carefully

   _____

2. we heared the sound of feetsteps comin down the hallway

   _____

Past, present or future?

3. The championship game is coming up on Saturday. _____

4. Last year we lost by only two points. _____

Circle the words with the same sound as "ea" in "treat"

5. beat   bread   sea   realize   thread

Write sentence or not a sentence.

1. Made a big snowman in our backyard. _____

2. After the big snowstorm, we went outside. _____

Correct these sentences.

3. is you ready for the math quiz on tuesday asked dan

   _____

4. i has studied my number facts for hours i replied

   _____

Write the root word (base word) for:

5. enjoyable   _____

Name: _____

Correct these sentences.

1. the track at westwood high school are a great plase to run

_____

2. me and carl likes to go their after school four a few hours

_____

Circle the words that does not belong..

3. Superior   Erie   Atlantic   Huron   Ontario

4. maple   elm   oak   spruce   palm

What is this person's occupation?

5. Mr. Orson fixed the leaky pipes in our kitchen. _____

- -

Name: _____

Fact or *fiction*?

1. You can see icebergs off the coast of Newfoundland. _____

2. Canada is the oldest country in North America. _____

Correct these sentences.

3. last saturday, our family taked a hike to rock dunder

_____

4. at the top, we set at a tabel and eated our lunch.

_____

Circle the words that rhyme.

5. shoe   blue   doe   grew   sew

Name: _____

Write the word or words that best complete each sentence.

1. My brother and I _____ to Green Valley Camp last summer.

   went / going / gone

2. Of all the activities we did, we liked swimming the _____

   good / better / best

3. At night, we _____ around a big campfire.

   set / sit / sat

4. We _____ some scary stories from the leaders.

   herd / heard / heared

5. We also got to _____ marshmallows and make S'mores.

   toste / toest / toast

- -

Name: _____

Bonus Activity: Making Compound Words

Make *compound words* by adding one of these words to each of the words below. Then illustrate your answer.

| shine | suds | bow | boat | cake |

1. rain	2. sun	3. house	4. soap	5. pan

MY CANADA

British Columbia has more kinds of animals than any other province.

Name: _____

Explain the meaning of the underlined words.

1.   The horse could run <u>like the wind</u>. _____

Correct these sentences.

2.   we bought pencils crayons and markers at sam's supersave

_____

3.   the squirrel runned to the top of the tree in maggie's yard

_____

Write the correct *pronoun* to replace the underlined noun.

4.   <u>Hank and I</u> like to play baseball.   _____

5.   <u>Lucy</u> takes piano lessons with Mrs. Harper.   _____

- -

Name: _____

Correct these sentences.

1.   we seed a reinbow after the rein had stoped

_____

2.   my favourite colours are purple blue and green

_____

Write the *comparative* and the *superlative* forms of the adjectives.

3.   great   _____   _____

4.   funny   _____   _____

Fact or opinion?

5.   Buddy's Burgers are the best!   _____

SSR1146   ISBN: 9781771587327 © On The Mark Press

Correct these sentences.

1. gimme back my soccer ball screemed nancy

_____

2. we is gonna go to sea the new disney movie on saturday

_____

Circle the word that is spelled correctly.

3. basball   bassball   baseball   basebal

4. punkin   punpkin   pumkin   pumpkin

Common **noun or** *proper* **noun?**

5. ferris wheel   _____

Correct these sentences.

1. kenny rides hims bike to fast down that there streat

_____

2. the kittin washed its fase with its littel pa

_____

What part of the friendly letter is this?

3. 1946 Brandon Drive   _____

4. I hope you can visit this summer. We will have great fun! _____

Does the underlined adjective tell which one, what kind or how many?

5. The <u>old</u> horse just plodded along.   _____

Name: _____

Decide if the underlined parts have a *capitalization* error, a *punctuation* error, a *spelling* error, or *no mistake*.

1. I have a penpal who lives in <u>japan</u>.   _____

2. She writes very <u>intresting</u> letters to me.   _____

3. Her last letter said that she has a <u>suprise</u> for me. _____

4. I asked her about it but <u>she said it's a secret.</u>   _____

5. Great <u>news</u> She is coming to Canada to <u>visit me</u>   _____

Name: _____

Bonus Activity: Dictionary Detectives

Read the sentences below. Think about the meaning of the underlined word.

Check the dictionary if you need help.

Circle *YES* or *NO* to answer each question.

YES   NO   1. Can a <u>yak</u> bite you?

YES   NO   2. Is <u>cement</u> heavy?

YES   NO   3. Is an <u>aileron</u> found on a tractor?

YES   NO   4. Does <u>grotesque</u> mean the same as beautiful?

YES   NO   5. Does a <u>quintet</u> have six people?

MY CANADA

Nunavut means "Our land" in Inuktitut.
      Nunavut is the biggest province or territory in Canada.

SSR1146   ISBN: 9781771587327 © On The Mark Press

Name: _____

Write the contraction made from these two words.

1. would not   _____

Correct these sentences.

2. excuse me, sandy, whut time are it rite now

_____

3. wow, that were a vary close rase to the finnish

_____

Write the _pronoun_ that would replace the underlined noun.

4. <u>Jim</u> loves tuna sandwiches for lunch.   _____

5. He takes <u>tuna sandwiches</u> to school twice a week. _____

Name: _____

Complete the analogies.

1. Willy is to William as Joey is to _____

2. Sandy is to Sandra as Susie is to _____

Correct these sentences.

3. larry, please tern them lights off

_____

4. last friday, we goed shoping at the westgate mall

_____

Write one good sentence using this pair of homophones.

5. write, right _____

Name: _____

Number these words in alphabetical order.

1. ____paste   ____package   ____partner   ____palace   ____paper

Correct these sentences.

2. has you read the story called princess scarface

_____

3. meny ferry tails has an evil which and a good witch

_____

Write two words that rhyme with each word.

4. crown   _____   _____

5. nine   _____   _____

Name: _____

Circle the correct abbreviation for September.

1. sept.   Septem.   Sept.   Septmbr.

Correct these sentences.

2. remember to brang rubber boots for our hike to martin's marsh

_____

3. if the wheather is good, we will have a picknick their

_____

Write the root word for each word.

4. unlikely   _____

5. happiness   _____

    SSR1146   ISBN: 9781771587327 © On The Mark Press

Name: _____

Which reference source would be best to find information for these things? Write *encyclopedia*, *dictionary*, *thesaurus*, *cookbook*, or *telephone book*.

1. foods that you might feed to a gerbil   _____

2. the meaning of the word "gazelle"   _____

3. information about the Great Lakes   _____

4. the number of the nearest library   _____

5. an antonym for the word "busy"   _____

Name: _____

Bonus Activity: Categories

Write the name of the category in the correct box in front of each list.

Things with wheels   Food for lunch   Things on a bed
Wild animals   Things used for writing

Name of Category			
1.	pillow	sheet	blanket
2.	fox	porcupine	skunk
3.	bike	roller skates	scooter
4.	sandwich	apple	cookies
5.	pencil	marker	pen

Alberta is Canada's sunniest province, with about 2000 hours of sunshine per year.

MY CANADA

Name: _____

Correct these sentences.

1. what does you do in your spar time for fun

_____

2. i likes reading drawing and playing soccer with my frends

_____

How many syllables in this word?

3. Bonavista   _____

Write a *common noun* for each proper noun.

4. Toronto Blue Jays   _____

5. Big Ben   _____

- -

Name: _____

Correct these sentences.

1. my sister are gonna be a nerse when her grows up

_____

2. i wants to be scientist who travels to canada's north

_____

Give two words that rhyme with each of these words.

3. grand   _____   _____

4. down   _____   _____

What do these words have in common?

5. hammer, nails, wood, saw   _____

SSR1146   ISBN: 9781771587327 © On The Mark Press

Name: _____

Write the two words that make up each contraction.

1. they've   _____   _____

2. I'd   _____   _____

Correct these sentences.

3. who is the author of the cat in the hat asked tracey

_____

4. i'm not gonna get no needel today screemed polly

_____

Tell if these words are *synonyms*, *antonyms* or *homophones*.

5. battle, fight   _____

Name: _____

Correct these sentences.

1. i am gonna ask henry jamie and zeke to play baskitball

_____

2. we has sum secrit plays we like to try on the other teem

_____

Write the *pronoun* that would replace the underlined words.

3. Mom is cooking spaghetti for supper tonight.   _____

4. Spaghetti is one of my favourite foods.   _____

Use context clues to determine the meaning of the underlined word.

5. The scientist discovered a remedy for chickenpox.   _____

Name: _____

Circle the verb that correctly completes each sentence.

1. The principal (**speaks / spoke**) to us yesterday.

2. The ice has (**freezes / frozen**) on our pond.

3. I will try to (**find / found**) your lost mittens.

4. Wally (**choose / chose**) to stay at home today.

5. Our school bell (**rung / rings**) at the same time each morning.

- -

Name: _____

Bonus Activity: Name Those Nouns!

Nouns are words that name a person, place or thing.

Read the words in the boxes. If the word is a *noun*, colour the box *light blue*.

sister	grows	help	bedroom	aunt
tells	leaves	apples	runs	looks
teacher	think	walk	boots	street

MY CANADA

The world's smallest desert is called the Carcross Desert, and is found in the Yukon Territory.

SSR1146   ISBN: 9781771587327 © On The Mark Press

Name: _____

Replace the underlined proper noun with a *pronoun*.

1. <u>Sarah</u> is my best friend.   _____

2. <u>Montreal</u> is a big city.   _____

Circle the correct abbreviation for November.

3.   NV   Nv.   Nov.   Novmbr.   Novbr.

Correct these sentences.

4.   on rainy daze, we likes to sit and red a book

_____

5.   witch basball teem is your favorite asked ben

_____

Name: _____

***Sentence* or *not a sentence*?**

1.   Overnight at my house?   _____

Correct these sentences.

2.   the atlantic ocean can be dangrous when its windy

_____

3.   fisherman have a hard life on rough sees

_____

Write the plural form of the following nouns.

4.   puppy   _____

5.   church   _____

Name: _____

How many syllables in this word?

1. Charlottetown _____

Circle the *pronouns* in each sentence.

2. He will take me with him to the beach.

3. She likes it so much she will keep it.

Correct these sentences.

4. we is going to canada's wonderland this august said jenny

_____

5. does you has a favorite ride i asked

_____

Name: _____

***Present*, *past* or *future*?**

1. I loved that movie, didn't you? _____

2. Let's take Molly to see it on Saturday. _____

Correct these sentences.

3. does you think therd grade are hard asked helen

_____

4. we'll has to lisen and werk hard answered mya

_____

Write two words that rhyme with the following word.

5. feather _____   _____

SSR1146   ISBN: 9781771587327 © On The Mark Press

Name: _____

Write "**and**" or "**but**" on the line to complete each sentence correctly.

1. A skunk has black fur _____ a white stripe on its back and tail.

2. It is not dangerous _____ you should stay away from one.

3. Skunks sleep during the day _____ they hunt at night.

4. If you startle it _____ scare it, it may spray you.

5. A skunk has short legs _____ it can move quickly.

Name: _____

Bonus Activity: Where's the Action?

Verbs are words that show *action*. **Read the words in the boxes. If the word is a verb, colour the box yellow.**

says	helps	school	pencil	smiled
write	flower	cried	roared	mittens
friend	thinks	ran	town	took

The Royal Canadian Mounted Police's Musical Ride started in Regina.

MY CANADA

SSR1146   ISBN: 9781771587327 © On The Mark Press

51

Name: _____

Where would this event likely happen?

1. I dribbled the ball down the field and took a shot on the net. _____

Tell if the underlined word is a *noun* or a *verb*.

2. Our <u>computer</u> is broken. _____

3. My grandmother <u>lives</u> in Grand Falls. _____

Correct these sentences.

4. has you ever read the book called haunted canada

_____

5. it have sum of the scarier storys i has read

_____

Name: _____

Fact or opinion?

1. Wheat is the main crop grown in Saskatchewan. _____

Write two words that rhyme with each of the following words.

2   went   _____   _____

3   dawn   _____   _____

Correct these sentences.

4. each provence in canada has its own flag and flour

_____

5. does you know witch street della lives on asked rick

_____

SSR1146   ISBN: 9781771587327 © On The Mark Press

Name: _____

Divide each word into syllables.

1.   mountainous   _____

2.   overboard   _____

Add a suffix to make a new word.

3.   call   _____

Correct these sentences.

4.   what time do the movie began asked tyler

_____

5.   does you mean adventures of the lost world replied jane

_____

- -

Name: _____

Correct these sentences.

1.   she knowed that her were gonna be in trouble

_____

2.   i breaked my mom's best dish yestarday

_____

Tell if these nouns are _common_ or _proper_.

3.   tractor   _____

4.   Robert Munsch   _____

Write the singular form of this noun.

5.   leaves   _____

Name: _____

Combine the two sentences into one good sentence.

1. Apples are fruits. Bananas are fruit. Oranges are fruits.

_____

2. Cows live on a farm. Horses live on a farm. Chickens live on a farm.

_____

3. Tomatoes grow in the garden. And so do green beans.

_____

4. You can see ocean for miles. Sometimes you see an ocean liner.

_____

5. Canada's north is a cold, harsh place. Very few people live there.

_____

- -

Name: _____

Bonus Activity: Canada Birds Word Search

Find and circle the following words in the puzzle.

loon	blue jay
puffin	wren
robin	cardinal
swan	crow
chickadee	
Canada goose	

c	a	r	d	i	n	a	l	i	t	r
f	h	b	h	c	c	m	l	o	h	o
t	n	i	f	f	u	p	r	o	f	b
f	c	r	c	h	a	w	c	s	o	i
a	d	b	h	k	b	t	s	w	a	n
b	l	u	e	j	a	y	i	t	c	t
c	s	o	f	m	s	d	y	s	a	o
l	c	r	o	w	c	n	e	r	w	n
i	a	c	h	p	v	f	p	e	l	t
c	a	n	a	d	a	g	o	o	s	e

MY CANADA

Some of the many lakes in northern Manitoba have never been named.

SSR1146   ISBN: 9781771587327 © On The Mark Press

Name: _____

Correct these sentences.

1. gimme that there socker ball so we can play a game

_____

2. we saw the prime minister in ottawa last july

_____

Write the root word for these words.

3. overdoing   _____

4. trickster   _____

Circle the words that have the same sound as "*ough*" in "enough".

5.   thought   tough   though   rough   cough

Name: _____

Does the underlined adjective tell *which one*, *what kind*, or *how many*?

1. My <u>older</u> brother plays basketball on his high school team. _____

Correct these sentences.

2. my baby brother, lewis, will be won on april 10, 2016

_____

3. him wants chocklate cup cakes insted of a birthday cake

_____

What do these words have in common?

4. run, skip, hop, sprint   _____

5. tulip, daffodil, crocus, snowdrop   _____

Name: _____

Tell if the underlined word is a *noun*, *verb* or *adjective*.

1. It was raining hard <u>last</u> night. _____

2. There were <u>puddles</u> everywhere this morning. _____

Circle the word that is spelled correctly.

3. frend   frand   freind   friend

Correct these sentences.

4. we gotta by apples cookies and juice boxes

_____

5. marianne is gonna bee late for her lesson

_____

Name: _____

***Fact* or *opinion*?**

1. Early explorers came here from England and France. _____

2. I think everyone should visit Banff National Park. _____

Correct these sentences.

3. joey he dont want to go too bed erly tonight

_____

4. we listened to the story lighthouse in the fog

_____

Write an *synonym* for each word.

5. bent _____   safe _____

SSR1146   ISBN: 9781771587327 © On The Mark Press

Name: _____

Combine these sentences to make one good sentence.

1. I lost my new jacket. I lost it on the bus. I lost it yesterday.

   _____

2. We hiked along the trail. We hiked for three hours. Then we stopped for lunch.

   _____

3. Would you like a hot dog? Do you like mustard on it? Do you like ketchup?

   _____

4. My cookies are gone. I think my brother took them. I see a trail of crumbs.

   _____

5. There are dark clouds in the sky. I think there will be a storm. It will begin soon.

   _____

- -

Name: _____

Bonus Activity: Idioms

Idioms are expressions that do not mean exactly what they seem to say.
Example: "all tied up" means "busy right now".

Draw a line to match each idiom with the correct meaning.

1. clear as mud •   • sound asleep

2. walking on air •   • be quiet; stop talking

3. bite your tongue •   • not understood

4. spill the beans •   • very happy or excited

5. out like a light •   • tell a secret

MY CANADA   *Each Canadian eats an average of 150 eggs per year.*

Name: _____

Tell if these word pairs are *antonyms*, *homophones* or *synonyms*.

1. lucky, fortunate _____

2. forward, backward _____

Correct these sentences.

3. our teem losed the finell game against the rockwood raiders

_____

4. i wants chocoklate syrup sprinkles and peanuts on my sundae

_____

Tell if the underlined word is a *noun*, *pronoun* or *verb*.

5. Mom <u>told</u> us she would pick us up at 8:00 P.M. _____

Name: _____

Use context clues to explain the meaning of the underlined word.

1. My sister wears the newest styles because she wants to be in <u>fashion</u>.

_____

2. My cousin does weird and funny things. We call him "<u>zany</u> Zack"

_____

Correct these sentences.

3. can you tell me where to hang this picture asked uncle jim

_____

4. me and my sister will walk to carrie's house on pineview street

_____

Write *sentence* or *not a sentence*.

5. The time of the show _____

 SSR1146   ISBN: 9781771587327 © On The Mark Press

Name: _____

Correct these sentences.

1. gabby said i think you should finish your work now

_____

2. we lisened to the song home again on the radeo

_____

Tell whether the underlined word has a *prefix* or a *suffix*.

3. Please <u>untie</u> the knots in your shoelace.   _____

4. Walk <u>carefully</u> on the icy street.   _____

In what part of the friendly letter would you find the following word?

5. Your cousin, Piper   _____

Name: _____

Number these words in alphabetical order.

1. ____ fish   ____ fight   ____ fixture   ____ field   ____ five

Correct these sentences.

2. i cant find mine keys anywheres said mom

_____

3. me thinks me saw them on the table in the hall i offered

_____

Where would these events likely take place?

4. New plants were sprouting up out of the ground. _____

5. The skater went to centre ice, bowed and began to skate.

_____

Name: _____

Homophones sound the same but they are spelled differently and have different meanings. **Write the correct homophone on the line to complete each sentence.**

1. Listen _____ this adventure story.
   (two / to / too)

2. Did you _____ the fans cheering for him?
   (hear / here)

3. This music is _____ loud for me.
   (two / to / too)

4. _____ going to come _____ for a visit.
   (Their / There / They're)   (hear / here)

5. _____ is _____ new car.
   (Their / There / They're)   (their / there / they're)

Name: _____

Bonus Activity: Analogies

Read the beginning of each analogy and then write the correct word to complete it.

Analogy
1. Head is to hat as foot is to
2. Tablecloth is to table as blanket is to
3. Water is to ocean as sand is to
4. Night is to moon as day is to
5. In is to out as white is to

MY CANADA

Polar bears grow long hair on the bottom of their paws to keep their feet warm and to give them a better grip on the ice.

          SSR1146   ISBN: 9781771587327 © On The Mark Press

Name: _____

Correct these sentences.

WEEK
19
ACTIVITY
1
TOTAL
/5

1. did you here yore sister callin you to dinner

_____

2. school start at 915 a m sharp each day

_____

What is this person probably doing?

3. Put water in the tub. Don't forget to use soap! _____

Give an antonym for each word.

4. soft _____

5. sunny _____

Name: _____

Circle the words that have the same sound as "u" in "pupil"

WEEK
19
ACTIVITY
2
TOTAL
/5

1. rules   but   amuse   value   funny   human

Correct these sentences.

2. the pitcher on that there postcard are beautiful

_____

3. we gived mom sum flowers for mother's day

_____

***Present*, *past* or *future*?**

4. I got my kitten, Boots, four years ago. _____

5. She will be five years old on February 10, 2016. _____

Name: _____

Number the words in alphabetical order.

1. ____ blast   ____ bleak   ____ black   ____ blind   ____ blend

Is the underlined part the *subject* or the *predicate* of the sentence?

2. <u>The puppet show</u> entertained the children.   _____

3. The puppets <u>danced and sang on the little stage</u>.   _____

Correct these sentences.

4. i left my knew jacket at the playview park last saturday

_____

5. we seed a reinbow after the storm on thursday

_____

Name: _____

Who might be saying the following?

1. "It's time for a bath and then to bed."   _____

2. "Tomorrow we will have a test on these words."_____

Circle the word that is spelled correctly.

3.   theef   theif   thief   thefe   thiefe

Correct these sentences.

4. which movie did you like bestest, frozen or zootopia

_____

5. we colleckted aggs at uncle harry's farm last sunday

_____

   SSR1146   ISBN: 9781771587327 © On The Mark Press

Underline the *compound word* in each sentence. Then write the two words that make up each compound word.

1.   How old will Polly be on her birthday? _____ _____

2.   Every afternoon my baby brother has a nap.

     _____ _____

3.   We are decorating our classroom for Parent Night.

     _____ _____

4.   Let's play downstairs in the family room. _____ _____

5.   Jeff can really go fast on his skateboard. _____ _____

- -

Name: _____

Bonus Activity: Listen to the Sound

Choose a word from the box that describes the sound each thing makes.

1. The wind   _____ .

2. Bacon   _____ .

3. Fire   _____ .

4. The telephone   _____ .

5. Thunder   _____ .

6. The train   _____ .

| whistles |
| rings |
| rumbles |
| howls |
| crackles |
| sizzles |

One of the world's best dinosaur museum   **MY CANADA**

is the Royal Tyrrell Museum in Drumheller, Alberta.

Complete the *analogy*.

1. Giant is to tall as elf is to _____

Give two words that rhyme with each of the following words.

2. round   _____   _____

3. cold   _____   _____

Correct these sentences.

4. our family has went to cape spear in newfoundland

_____

5. youse can see the city of st john's and the harbour

_____

Correct these sentences.

1. we is gonna order pizza from pizza plus on friday night

_____

2. for desert we will has ice cream sandwitches

_____

How many syllables in each word?

3. dictionary   _____

4. imagination   _____

Write a *common noun* for the proper noun.

5. Calgary Flames   _____

SSR1146   ISBN: 9781771587327 © On The Mark Press

Name: _____

Write the correct abbreviation for:

1. Royal Canadian Mounted Police   _____

Correct these sentences.

2. dont ferget to pick up yore toys called mom

_____

3. we has lived in cornwall, ontario for too years

_____

Write the two words used to make each contraction.

4. doesn't   _____   _____

5. he'll   _____   _____

Name: _____

Write the _root word_ for each of these words.

1. unpainted   _____

2. hopelessly   _____

Correct these sentences.

3. we want for a picknick in woodland park on sunday

_____

4. sum ants cralled onto the tabel and headed for the foode

_____

Circle the word that does not belong.

5. crayons   markers   erasers   coloured pencils

Name: _____

Write the correct word on the line to complete each sentence.

1. _____ and _____ are going to play on the soccer team.
(I / me / Rob)

2. Some of our friends are going to join _____ and _____ .
(him / me)

3. _____ and _____ had a great time! (I / me / Rob)

4. The coach showed _____ and _____ some good moves.
(me / him)

5. _____ and _____ were proud of what we had learned.
(I / me / Rob)

Name: _____

Bonus Activity: Dictionary Detectives

Read the words. Check the meaning in the dictionary. Circle the correct meaning from the choices.

1. **aroma**: taste   idea   smell   sound   picture

2. **couple**: four   six   two   ten   one

3. **grip**: tie up   paint   hide   grasp   tell

4. **magnify**: get shorter   get bigger   get sweeter   get smaller

5. **raw**: not sweet   not sour   not cooked   not salty

6. **scamper**: swim   talk   write   jump   run

The Great Lakes make up the largest body of fresh water in the world.
MY CANADA

Name: _____

Write the correct *possessive form* for these expressions.

1.   the new puppy belongs to Selena   _____

2.   the truck belonging to my dad   _____

Correct these sentences.

3.   what colour is yore faverite asked pete

_____

4.   definitely, i like read the bestest i replied

_____

Write the root word for:

5.   moisture   _____

WEEK
21

ACTIVITY
1

TOTAL
/5

Name: _____

Correct these sentences.

1.   becuz it are snowing, our buss will arrive late for school

_____

2.   the bell rungs at 910 am sharpe evry morning

_____

Give two words that rhyme with each of these words.

3.   loud   _____   _____

4.   gift   _____   _____

Tell where this event is happening.

5.   When the bell rang, the children ran to line up.   _____

WEEK
21

ACTIVITY
2

TOTAL
/5

Name: _____

Circle the word that is spelled correctly.

1. chepmunk   chipmonke   chipmunk   chapmunk

Correct these sentences.

2. we is doing a play called the lonely christmas tree fore our parants

_____

3. our teacher, miss drake, are bringin is a hug tree fore us

_____

Fact or *fantasy?*

4. If you find the end of a rainbow, you will see a pot of gold coins. _____

5. A rainbow forms when it rains as the sun shines. _____

Name: _____

Correct these sentences.

1. we is reeding a book called ramona the pest in hour class

_____

2. some peeple likes the stroy, but others dont

_____

Write "k" or "ch" to tell the sound of "ch" in these words.

3. stoma<u>ch</u>   _____

4. <u>ch</u>ocolate   _____

Write and *antonym* for this word.

5. cloudy   _____

   SSR1146   ISBN: 9781771587327 © On The Mark Press

Name: _____

What reference source would be best to find information for these things? Write *encyclopedia*, *dictionary*, *thesaurus*, *cookbook*, or *telephone book*.

1. how to make a chocolate cake _____

2. the meaning of the word "crisis" _____

3. the habitat of the beaver _____

4. the number of the nearest hospital _____

5. a synonym for the word "speedy" _____

Name: _____

Bonus Activity: Canadian Critters

Read clues. Choose the correct word from the Word Box to match the clue. Write the word by putting one letter in each space.

rabbit	raccoon	seal	skunk	squirrel

Clues							
1	I love to swim and dive.						
2	My friends might call me "Stinky".						
3	I can hop away very quickly.						
4	I like to hunt for my food at night.						
5	Watch me scurry along a tree branch.						

The world's biggest Easter egg can be seen in Vegreville, Alberta. **MY CANADA**

Name: _____

Fact or *opinion*?

1. Everyone loves the snow! _____

2. Big ships sail up the St. Lawrence River. _____

Circle the word that comes first alphabetically.

3. infant   incorrect   include   inch   insect

Correct these sentences.

4. hallie has broke all her knew crayons and pensils

    _____

5. we aint gots enough time to finish our werk before lunch

    _____

Name: _____

Tell how many syllables are in this word.

1. thunderstorm _____

Write the *pronoun* for the underlined words.

2. <u>Tony and Amy</u> are my cousins. _____

3. <u>Ed</u> hit a home run in the final game. _____

Correct these sentences.

4. has you ever red the magazine called just for kids

    _____

5. it have lotsa good infermation jokes and puzzles

    _____

SSR1146   ISBN: 9781771587327 © On The Mark Press

Name: _____

Complete these *analogies*.

1. Antlers are to deer as tusks are to_____

2. Milk is to cow as egg is to_____

Circle the word that is spelled correctly

3. toste   toaste   tost   toast   taost

Correct these sentences.

4. sumone leaved the lite on all nite in the kitchen

_____

5. i likes to play the game, apples, with my frends

_____

Name: _____

Tell what this person's job would be.

1. She protects us and makes sure people obey the law. _____

Correct these sentences.

2. who are in charge of this here job asked mr miller

_____

3. we taked meny pitchers when we was at niagara falls, ontario

_____

Use context clues to explain the meaning of the underlined words.

4. It makes me <u>irate</u> when my brother touches my things

_____

5. The <u>citizens</u> of our town are voting today.

_____

Name: _____

Combine these sentences to make one good, longer sentence.

1. I love to swim. I like to swim at the beach. I like swimming on hot days.

    _____

2. My friend is Gary. Gary is coming over. We are going to play video games.

    _____

3. I am having a party. It is a birthday party. It will be on Saturday.

    _____

4. We watched the parade. It had clowns doing tricks. It had a marching band.

    _____

5. My kitten is named Poppy. She washes her face. She uses her paws.

    _____

- -

Name: _____

Bonus Activity: What's the Time?

Read each sentence. Write *present*, *past* or *future* to tell *when* each event takes place.

1. I wanted that new jacket very much.   _____

2. Everyone thinks our test will be easy.   _____

3. We ate every piece of cake on the plate.   _____

4. You will be a great runner because you practise.   _____

5. I was thrilled to get my award.   _____

There are more than 10,000 glaciers on Baffin Island. Brrrr!!   **MY CANADA**

SSR1146 ISBN: 9781771587327 © On The Mark Press

Correct these sentences.

1. i'm grumpy i need a nap said grandpa

_____

2. would you like me to make you a cup of tee i asked

_____

Use context clues to explain the meaning of the underlined word.

3. We could see a candle flicker in the window. _____

Circle the word that comes first in alphabetical order.

4.   hilly   hint   hide   hiccup   hitch

5.   radish   railway   raccoon   rather   rascal

Correct these sentences.

1. becuz it were reiny outside, we didnt play in the yard

_____

2. thats a great pair of soccer cleets said coach brock

_____

Past, present, or future?

3. My sister is getting married in July. _____

4. Mom went shopping for groceries last night. _____

Write the contraction made from these two words.

5. does not   _____

Name: _____

Correct these sentences.

1. this here salad has lettuce cucumbers and tomatoes in it

   _____

2. pedro are training hims dog to do too new tricks

   _____

Tell if these words are *synonyms* or *antonyms*.

3. defend, protect   _____

***Fact* or *opinion*?**

4. Cars always speed on our street.   _____

5. Milk is good for us.   _____

WEEK 23 ACTIVITY 3 TOTAL /5

Name: _____

In which part of a friendly letter would the following be found?

1. Dear Aunt Hilda   _____

Give *three* words that rhyme with each of these words.

2. back   _____

3. trick   _____

Correct these sentences.

4. doesnt he has too brothers and won sister

   _____

5. me and jillian wants to go to sea that there movie monsterville

   _____

WEEK 23 ACTIVITY 4 TOTAL /5

SSR1146   ISBN: 9781771587327 © On The Mark Press

Name: _____

Decide if the underlined parts have a *capitalization* error, a *punctuation* error, a *spelling* error or *no mistake*.

1. Long ago people could not study <u>natchure</u> easily. _____

2. <u>they</u> were frightened when they heard thunder in the sky.

   _____

3. They made up stories <u>to explain thunder?</u> _____

4. <u>some</u> thought it was the gods who were angry. _____

5. <u>Today we know that lightning heating up the air causes thunder.</u>

   _____

- -

Name: _____

Bonus Activity: Baby Animals

Complete the puzzle using words from the Word Box.

Across
1. A baby deer is called a ____
2. A baby dog is called a ____
3. A baby cow is called a ____
4. A baby sheep is called a ____

Down
1. A baby horse is called a ____
2. A baby pig is called a ____
5. A baby goat is called a ____

| kid piglet fawn foal |
| pup calf lamb |

MY CANADA   *Quebec is Canada's #1 producer of maple syrup.*

Name: _____

Use context to explain the meaning of the underlined word in this sentence.

1.   My new puppy is <u>frisky</u>. She grabs my pant leg and pulls on it.

_____

Correct these sentences.

2.   this christmas we is goin to aunt jan's house in edmonton

_____

3.   will you learn me how to skipp double dutch

_____

Complete the *analogies*.

4.   snake is to hiss as duck is to _____

5.   hot is to fire as cold is to _____

- -

Name: _____

Add *two suffixes* to each of the following words.

1.   stop   _____   _____

2.   cry   _____   _____

Correct these sentences.

3.   me and my family is going to hour cottage on red lake

_____

4.   we goes fishing swimming and hikeing all the times

_____

Tell if this sentence is a *question*, *exclamation* or *command*.

5.   When will you be finished your homework? _____

SSR1146   ISBN: 9781771587327 © On The Mark Press

Name: _____

Underline the *subject* in the following sentence.

1. My brother and I are getting new bikes this summer.

Correct these sentences.

2. the grade 3 class perfromed a play called the friendly dragon

_____

3. evryone claped and cheered when the dragin saved the little boy

_____

Write the *pronoun* that would replace the underlined noun.

4. <u>Jason's</u> pony is named Star.   _____

5. <u>Star</u> is gentle and easy to train.   _____

- -

Name: _____

Correct these sentences.

1. how did this here plate get broken asked mom

_____

2. jenny brung her markers pensils and crayins to school

_____

Write the correct *abbreviation* for each word.

3. mister   _____

4. December   _____

Tell if the underlined word is a *noun*, *verb* or *adjective*.

5. My new shoes are very <u>shiny</u>.   _____

Name: _____

Write **S** for *statement* (tells a fact); **I** for *interrogative* (asks a question); **C** for *command* (ask someone to do something) and **E** for *exclamatory* (surprise or excitement).

1. Aren't these flowers beautiful?   _____

2. The ants are invading our picnic!   _____

3. Quick, move the food and the plates.   _____

4. It is very peaceful in the park.   _____

5. Would you like to stay here longer?   _____

Name: _____

Bonus Activity: Awesome Adverbs!

Adverbs are words that tell **how**, **when** or where something happens.

Colour the boxes that have words that are adverbs.

Hint: you should find seven adverbs.

softly	trains	easily	there
snow	early	here	circus
house	quietly	bird	later

The *first choclate bar* was made in New Brunswick in 1910 at the Gangong Candy Factory.

MY CANADA

SSR1146   ISBN: 9781771587327 © On The Mark Press

Correct these sentences.

Name: _____

1. does youse like chiken noodal soap and crackers

_____

2. i eats it for lunsh every saturday becuse mom make it

_____

Write the possessive nouns.

3. the books of the teacher _____

4. the pencils of the students _____

Write the two words used to make this contraction.

5. isn't _____ _____

- -

Name: _____

Correct these sentences.

1. me and max wants to help simon wash his bike on saturday

_____

2. simon are rideing hims bike in the parade

_____

Is this sentence a *statement*, *question*, *command* or *exclamation*?

3. Have you ever seen the Rocky Mountains? _____

How many syllables in each word?

4. Marystown _____

5. Shediac _____

Name: _____

Is the underlined word a *noun*, *verb*, *adjective* or *adverb*?

1. We face the <u>flag</u> when we sing O' Canada. _____

2. The hound dog <u>howled</u> as he followed the trail. _____

Correct these sentences.

3. lets meat at the playground at 630 pm to play socker

_____

4. bring yore frends monty and devon to play two

_____

Number these words in alphabetical order.

5. ___navy   ___napkin   ___nation   ___nature   ___nag

Name: _____

Correct these sentences.

1. will you ask ms wilson to help use with this here question

_____

2. how much muney do you has in your piggy banke

_____

Does the underlined adjective tell *what kind*, *how many* or *which one*?

3. The owl's <u>large</u> eyes help it to hunt at night. _____

Fact or *opinion*?

4. The best season in Canada is summer. _____

5. Gold is mined in the Yukon. _____

SSR1146   ISBN: 9781771587327 © On The Mark Press

Name: _____

Write the word that best completes the sentence.

1. We are taking _____ puppy to Dr. Willows our vet.

    (**our / hour / are**)

2. Having a _____ in your garden is a good thing.

    (**tode / towed / toad**)

3. Who _____ the most answers to the math quiz?

    (**knew / new / knowed**)

4. When is Tim's library book _____?

    (**dew / due / do**)

5. _____ moving to a new apartment soon.

    (**Their / They're / There**)

Name: _____

Bonus Activity: Smallest? Biggest?

Underline the word that *names the smallest object* in the group. *Circle* the word that *names the biggest object* in the group.

1. bicycle / airplane / bus / car / roller skates / train

2. cup / bowl / plate / glass / platter / spoon

3. bracelet / crown / ring / watch / necklace

4. teenager / baby / parent / toddler / Grade 3 student

5. body / finger / arm / leg / head / foot

6. toonie / quarter / dime / loonie / $5 bill

Nunavut has three official languages: Inuktituk, French and English.

MY CANADA

Present, past or *future*?

1. Our team won the championship game!   _____

2. Hank is going to Moncton this summer.   _____

Correct these sentences.

3. did you remember to pack your bathing suite goggles and swam fins

_____

4. i is so exsited to be going to sandbanks provincial park on saturday

_____

Complete the following *analogy*.

5. B is to letter as 9 is to _____

Synonyms or *antonyms*?

1. king, queen   _____

2. ruin, wreck   _____

Divide the word into syllables.

3. furniture   _____

Correct these sentences.

4. an earthquake hit japan and cause lottsa damage

_____

5. i hopes i gets to go with dad to the riverview annual boat show

_____

SSR1146   ISBN: 9781771587327 © On The Mark Press

Name: _____

Write the *pronoun* that would replace the underlined words.

1.   <u>Allan and I</u> cheered when our team scored a goal.   _____

2.   <u>Steven</u> will be picked up from school today.   _____

Correct these sentences.

3.   our class are going to the royal canadian mint in ottawa

_____

4.   has you ever bean to the top of the cn tower

_____

Write the *past tense* for the following verb.

5.   carry   _____

Name: _____

Correct these sentences.

1.   will you trade for quarters for a loonie asked ethan

_____

2.   we eats our lunch at 1140 am each day at scool

_____

Tell if the underlined word is a *noun*, *verb*, *adjective* or *adverb*.

3.   Gord <u>disagreed</u> with my answer.   _____

4.   The butterfly floated <u>gracefully</u> among the flowers.   _____

Write a good sentence using this pair of homophones

5.   hair, hare   _____

Name: _____

What reference source would be best to find information for these things?
Write *encyclopedia*, dictionary, *thesaurus*, *cookbook*, or *telephone book*.

1. another word for "smart" _____

2. information about the building of the first railroad _____

3. the number of the nearest Tim Horton's shop _____

4. the meaning of the word " fortress" _____

5. how long to cook chocolate chip cookies _____

Name: _____

Bonus Activity: What Shall I Wear?

Think about what each person might wear while doing their job.
Circle the words that best completes each sentence.

1. A lumberjack would wear (a straw hat / safety boots / shorts and sandals)

2. A fairy tale princess would wear (a leather jacket / hiking boots / a fancy dress)

3. A fireman would wear (running shoes / a fireproof suit / a necklace)

4. A baker would wear (a swim suit / a winter coat / a white coat and hat)

5. A soldier would wear (a camouflage suit / a red silk hat / fancy shoes)

6. A policeman would wear (shorts and T-shirt / rubber boots / dark uniform)

MY CANADA

Kids around the world eat bread made from wheat grown in Saskatchewan.

SSR1146   ISBN: 9781771587327 © On The Mark Press

Name: _____

Correct these sentences.

1. wes, yore a great runner exclaimed troy

_____

2. i hope it dont rein on sunday and spoil our picknick

_____

Write the two words that make up each contractions.

3. shouldn't   _____   _____

4. he's   _____   _____

Circle the word that comes first alphabetically.

5.   powder   poke   polish   polecat   pout

Name: _____

Write the *plural form* of each noun.

1. tooth   _____

2. box   _____

Write the number of syllables in this word.

3. Geraldton   _____

Correct these sentences.

4. i needs to shop for rein boots befor spring gets hear

_____

5. aunt rose have went to see dr martins because her feeled sick

_____

Name: _____

Use context clues to explain the meaning of the underlined words.

1. Check your work to make sure your answers are <u>accurate</u>.

    _____

2. That hail storm will <u>devastate</u> our crop of wheat. _____

Correct these sentences.

3. my favorit puppy is the all black won said casey

    _____

4. maybee you cud name it snowball i joked

    _____

Does the underlined adjective tell *how many*, *which one*, or *what kind*?

5. I have invited <u>several</u> friends to my birthday party. _____

Name: _____

Write three words that rhyme with "*head*".

1. _____   _____   _____

Correct these sentences.

2. canada are a part of the continint of north america

    _____

3. hector are gonna bee late if him don't hurry up

    _____

Circle the *nouns* in each sentence.

4. My sister likes strawberries, blueberries and raspberries.

5. The pet shop sells birds, gerbils and hamsters.

   SSR1146   ISBN: 9781771587327 © On The Mark Press

Name: _____

Circle the letters that should be *capitalized*. Put *periods*, *question marks* and *exclamation marks* where they are needed.

1. mr and mrs campbell moved to kitchener ___

2. did ben take a picture of that huge maple tree ___

3. charlotte won the first prize for drawing ___

4. oh, david, what a mess you have made ___

5. who is going with you to Oshawa on saturday ___

Name: _____

Bonus Activity: In My Classroom, You will Find...

Find and circle the following words in the puzzle.

books	scissors	paint
chair	teacher	pencils
chalk	desk	ruler
computer	blackboard	
crayons	glue	

a	m	c	s	k	o	o	b	s	c
d	g	h	i	h	d	f	y	h	l
b	l	a	c	k	b	o	a	r	d
m	u	i	l	a	f	l	p	y	e
i	e	r	a	f	k	g	e	c	s
t	n	c	r	a	y	o	n	s	k
r	e	t	u	p	m	o	c	a	m
r	u	l	e	r	t	n	i	a	p
r	e	h	c	a	e	t	l	s	w
s	c	i	s	s	o	r	s	b	h

MY CANADA

Winnie-the-Pooh was named after a real bear that had been named after the city of Winnipeg.

Name: _____

Underline the *cause* and *circle* the *effect* in each sentence.

1. I am wearing my mittens because it is cold out today.

2. If you waste time, you will be late.

Correct these sentences.

3. terry has broke anuther window with hims football

_____

4. my cousen, kelly, have a knew baby girl named quinn

_____

Write the present tense of the underlined verb in this sentence.

5. Adele <u>told</u> us she would help us with our math.   _____

- -

Name: _____

Where would the following probably take place?

1. Pick up your order at the second window, please. _____

Correct these sentences.

2. does you think youse will be abel to go with us on friday

_____

3. we watched the land that time forgot last night on tv

_____

Fact or *opinion*?

4. Connor really needs to get a hair cut.   _____

5. Australia is the smallest continent.   _____

     SSR1146   ISBN: 9781771587327 © On The Mark Press

Name: _____

Is the *subject* or the *predicate* underlined in these sentences?

1. <u>Tammy and her brother</u> want to go swimming. _____

2. The Jeffersons <u>bought a new house in Banff</u>. _____

Present, past, or future?

3. You will be in grade four next year. _____

Correct these sentences.

4. in math, we add subtract multiply and divide

_____

5. mother cat take good cair of her babys and keep them save

_____

Name: _____

Complete the *analogy*.

1. radio is to listen as television is to _____

Correct these sentences.

2. your not lookin at the rite page in yore book

_____

3. my dad like most sports but him like golf the bestest

_____

Circle the *adverbs* in these sentences

4. The car drove quickly and carelessly down our street.

5. The fans cheered loudly for the home team.

Name: _____

Decide if the underlined parts have a *capitalization* error, a *punctuation* error, a *spelling* error, or *no mistake*.

1.   Leanne was very sad because her family <u>was moveing</u>.

_____

2.   Why did they have <u>to move at this time of year</u>   _____

3.   <u>She decided to take one last walk along her street.</u>   _____

4.   <u>she</u> tried hard not to cry as she walked along   _____

5.   Her friends were waiting when she returned. <u>What a surprise</u>

_____

Name: _____

Bonus Activity: What Grows in My Garden?

Write the correct name of the vegetable that matches each clue.

| beet   carrot   cucumber   peas   potatoes   tomatoes |

1. I grow underground. You can use me to make French fries.   _____

2. I grow under the ground. I am long and orange.   _____

3. I grow in a pod. My plant likes to climb.   _____

4. I grow under the ground. I am purple-red in colour.   _____

5. I grow on a bushy plant. You can use me to make ketchup.   _____

6. I grow on a vine. You can use me to make pickles.   _____

The province of Quebec was completely covered by glaciers during the Ice Age.

MY CANADA

SSR1146   ISBN: 9781771587327 © On The Mark Press

Name: _____

Correct these sentences.

1. me and elise dont got no reeding homework tonite

_____

2. kenny gots a knew job at the supersuds car wash

_____

Singular or *plural* noun?

3. feet   _____

4. dragons   _____

Command, *exclamation*, *question*, or *statement*?

5. Pick up all your toys on your bedroom floor. _____

Name: _____

Correct these sentences.

1. reagan, why wasn't you at school yesterday asked pam

_____

2. the read car comed speedin down brock street

_____

Use context clues to explain the meaning of the underlined words.

3. We <u>reside</u> at 199 Holland Avenue. _____

4. Grandma's best glasses are made of <u>crystal</u>. _____

Write the past tense for this verb.

5. hear   _____

Name: _____

Correct these sentences.

1. them chattering squirels like to run hi in hour trees

_____

2. i wont be in the rase tomorrow because i hert my ankel

_____

Common or *proper* **noun?**

3. Bay of Fundy   _____

4. shipwreck   _____

Write all the adjectives in this sentence.

5. Who owns this blue and yellow scarf? _____

Name: _____

Write the *root* or *base* word for these words.

1. farthest   _____

2. hopping   _____

Correct these sentences.

3. me and sadie is going to the grocerry store to gets pizza dough

_____

4. we allso needs pepperoni cheese and tomatoe sauce

_____

Divide this word into syllables.

5. familiar   _____

SSR1146   ISBN: 9781771587327 © On The Mark Press

Name: _____

Combine the two sentences to make one good sentence.

1. We went to the petting zoo. We fed the animals.

_____

2. The dandelion seeds floated away. It was very windy.

_____

3. Lizards are reptiles. They are cold-blooded.

_____

4. You did a great science project. You should be proud of yourself.

_____

5. You can make things in the sand. You can build a castle or a wall.

_____

Name: _____

Bonus Activity: Canada Birds Unscramble

Unscramble these words to correctly spell the names of Canadian birds.

1. uelb yaj   _____   5. wwlloas   _____

2. eechdacki   _____   6. lanidrac   _____

3. obrni   _____   7. eongip   _____

4. allsegu   _____   8. ffpuin   _____

MY CANADA *Forests cover over 80% of all land in New Brunswick.*

Fact or *fiction?*

1. Ellen's fire safety poster is the best! _____

Correct these sentences.

2. rideing the roller coaster is fun, isnt it

_____

3. canadians celebrate thanksgiving day in october

_____

Circle the word that does not belong in the group.

4. baseball   basketball   ocean   hockey

5. circle   triangle   square   yellow

WEEK

30

ACTIVIT

1

TOTAL

/5

Synonyms or *antonyms?*

1. sob, weep   _____

Correct these sentences.

2. me and freddie have did all the dishes

_____

3. jed has ate his sandwitch and drunk hims milk

_____

Write number of syllables in each word.

4. information   _____

5. assembly   _____

WEEK

30

ACTIVI

2

TOTAL

/5

SSR1146   ISBN: 9781771587327 © On The Mark Press

Name: _____

Correct these sentences.

1. is we goona go fishin on saturday grandpa

_____

2. them crickets was cherping loudly all nite

_____

Write the _root_ (base) word for:

3. reheated   _____

Number these words in alphabetical order.

4. ____ flap   ____ flare   ____ flash   ____ flag

5. ____ orbit   ____ ore   ____ orange   ____ order

- -

Name: _____

Correct these sentences.

1. who rote the book the mouse and the motorcycle

_____

2. we walk our dog, rico, evry nite after dinner

_____

Present , _past_ or _future_?

3. Will my birthday ever get here?   _____

Underline the _predicate_ in each sentence.

4. We visited our grandmother in Hamilton.

5. Jenny and her sister help their neighbour every Saturday.

Name: _____

Complete each sentence by writing the correct word on the line.

1. The bus _____ arrived on time. (**have / was / has**)

2. Karlee and _____ are going shopping at the new mall. (**me / I / us**)

3. You did much _____ work this time. (**gooder / better / well**)

4. Sue _____ bought a new umbrella. (**have / had / has**)

5. We _____ a double rainbow in the sky. (**seen / saw / seed**)

- -

Name: _____

Bonus Activity: Yum!!

Canadians have their favourite treats to eat. **Write the words under the correct heading.**

| maple syrup | beaver tails | poutine | French toast |
| apples | mac and cheese | | |

Two Syllable Treats	Three Syllable Treats	Four Syllable Treats

MY CANADA *Wild ponies live on Sable Island. It is an island close to Nova Scotia.*

SSR1146   ISBN: 9781771587327 © On The Mark Press

Name: _____

Circle the word that is spelled correctly.

1. reely   realy   relly   really

2. frend   freind   friend   frind

Correct these sentences.

3. it were a accident wen i breaked the old dish

_____

4. kim live at the corner of queen and elm streets

_____

Write the *present tense* for this verb.

5. said   _____

- -

Name: _____

Does the underlined adjective tell *which one*, *what kind* or *how many*?

1. My kite has <u>green</u> stripes on it.   _____

2. A <u>few</u> pages of my book are missing.   _____

Correct these sentences.

3. donnie dont like no vegetables but corn

_____

4. julie asked what time is we leaveing today

_____

Underline the *cause* and *circle* the *effect* in this sentence.

5. The bell rang so we lined up.

SSR1146   ISBN: 9781771587327 © On The Mark Press

What do the following words have in common?

1. Mercury   Venus   Earth   Mars   _____

2. ten   twenty   thirty   forty   _____

Present, *past* or *future*?

3. The play will start at 7:00 pm sharp.   _____

Correct these sentences.

4. i likes the story clifford the big red dog

_____

5. who sings that there song playin on the radio

_____

Does the adverb tell *where*, *when* or *how* something happened?

1. Nancy called her friend, Celia, <u>yesterday</u>.   _____

Correct these sentences.

2. does you believe that there story about the tigers

_____

3. does you like rainy or suny weather asked fanny

_____

Sentence or *not a sentence*?

4. Please close.   _____

5. Are you interested in helping him?   _____

    SSR1146   ISBN: 9781771587327 © On The Mark Press

Name: _____

Write the *contraction* that would replace the underlined words.

1. <u>He is</u> going camping this weekend. _____

2. I think <u>I will</u> go to bed now. _____

3. This math problem <u>is not</u> very hard to solve. _____

4. <u>There is</u> enough cookies for everyone. _____

5. <u>Let us</u> join in that game of soccer. _____

- -

Name: _____

Bonus Activity: Categories

Write a word for each category that begins with the letter given.

Letter	Names of Boys	Foods	Names of Girls	Animals
Bb				
Hh				
Mm				
Ss				

Cape Breton Island is home to over 500 bald eagles.   **MY CANADA**

Correct these sentences.

1.   does you know the way to the nearest hardwear store

_____

2.   we has ordered a large pizza from pizza palace

_____

Circle the words that have the same sound as "ow" in "now".

3.   crow   cow   grown   frown

Write an *synonym* for each word.

4.   beautiful   _____

5.   completed.   _____

- -

Name: _____

Where would the following probably take place?

1.   We boarded the plane and found our seats quickly.   _____

Correct these sentences.

2.   hour dog, spike, chewed my knew shoes

_____

3.   grandmas makeing me a new blew dress

_____

Underline the *subject* in each sentence.

4.   Dad hammered the boards into place.

5.   The old log cabin was Great Grandpa's first home.

        SSR1146   ISBN: 9781771587327 © On The Mark Press

Name: _____

Sentence or *not a sentence?*

1. The oldest boy. _____

2. My mother called me. _____

Correct these sentences.

3. dont be late for the game called coach jones

_____

4. our team wares blew and read shirts for each game

_____

Complete this *analogy*.

5. wing is to bird as fin is to _____

Name: _____

Underline the *subject* in this sentence.

1. Rachel and Ashley will sing a duet at the concert.

Correct these sentences.

2. i wont not ever touch them thistles agin

_____

3. me and you is gonna has a great time

_____

Write *three* words that rhyme with each word.

4. breeze _____

5. cross _____

Name: _____

Words can have more than one meaning. **Check the box of the sentence that matches the meaning.**

Meaning	Sentence 1	Sentence 2
board: to get on	❏ This <u>board</u> is made of oak.	❏ It's time to <u>board</u> the train.
felt: kind of cloth	❏ She <u>felt</u> sick today.	❏ The hat was made of <u>felt</u>.
trail: to follow	❏ My puppy <u>trails</u> behind me.	❏ That <u>trail</u> is for bikes.
patient: sick person	❏ The nurse helped the <u>patient</u>.	❏ Be <u>patient</u>; don't rush.
dash: a small amount	❏ Let's make a <u>dash</u> for it.	❏ Put in a <u>dash</u> of salt.

- -

Name: _____

Bonus Activity: A Not–So–Secret Message!

Discover the message by using the code below. Write the letter that comes alphabetically before each in the code.

The first one has been done to help you.

C															!
D	b	o	b	e	b		j	t		u	i	f		c	f	t	u	!

Prince Edward Island has no major rivers.   **MY CANADA**

SSR1146   ISBN: 9781771587327 © On The Mark Press

ANSWER KEY

WEEK 1: ACTIVITY 1

1. Do you like kittens or puppies best?
2. My sister and I like to help our mom.
3. able
4. ghost
5. near: answers will vary

WEEK 1: ACTIVITY 2

1. Not a sentence
2. Sentence
3. A good book to read is The Incredible Journey.
4. Mrs. Davis, our neighbour, bakes the best cookies.
5. Toronto Maple Leafs: proper noun

WEEK 1: ACTIVITY 3

1. Amazement, wonder
2. Have you ever travelled on a boat on Lake Ontario?
3. Jake wants to go to Toronto Metro Zoo.
4. win – ter
5. fid – dle

WEEK 1: ACTIVITY 4

1. elevator: 4
2. mountainous: 3
3. We is going to Pizza Palace for Ella's birthday.
4. I am buying her a great book called Ramona.
5. Fri.

WEEK 1: ACTIVITY 5

1. dictionary
2. cookbook
3. telephone book
4. encyclopedia
5. dictionary

BONUS ACTIVITY: NAMES THAT NEED CAPITALS

1. a weekday: Friday
2. a street: Main Street
3. our country: Canada
4. July 1: Canada Day
5. Canada's capital: Ottawa
6. a month: June

WEEK 2: ACTIVITY 1

1. The movie we want to watch is on TV at 7:30 on Tuesday.
2. Is your favourite holiday Easter or Thanksgiving?
3. don't: do not
4. they'll: they will/shall
5. cash, money: synonym

WEEK 2: ACTIVITY 2

1. carelessness: care
2. daily: day
3. fiction
4. "I used an atlas to locate the Gaspe," said Mike.
5. "Our family is going there in July," he added.

WEEK 2: ACTIVITY 3

1. Canadian coins
2. My sister Leah is too small to go down this slide.
3. What was the final score of the basketball game?
4. Dog is to bark as cow is to: moo
5. Glove is to hand as shoe is to: foot

WEEK 2: ACTIVITY 4

1. Will you cheer for the Oilers or the Flames in Saturday's game?
2. "My cousins both go to Briar Hill Middle School," said Jenny.
3. Your duty, obligation
4. Montreal Canadiens: hockey team
5. Patrick Chan: figure skater

WEEK 2: ACTIVITY 5

1. Monday, Tuesday, Wednesday: Thursday
2. spring summer, autumn: winter
3. five, ten, fifteen
4. day, week, month: year
5. first, second, third: fourth

BONUS ACTIVITY: TELL A STORY

2, 1, 3, 4

WEEK 3: ACTIVITY 1

1. He and I play on the same soccer team, the Tigers.
2. My sister, Susan, is getting married on August 21, 2016.
3. babies: plural
4. dress: singular
5. though, ghost, gold

WEEK 3: ACTIVITY 2

1. Sentence
2. Not a sentence
3. "Are the Rocky Mountains in British Columbia?" asked Pete.
4. We love the Easter egg hunt at Aunt May's each year.
5. The (beautiful) flowers are (red), (yellow) and (orange.)

WEEK 3: ACTIVITY 3

1. Canadian wild rodents
2. winter sports
3. "The Great Gilly Hopkins is a good story," said Ms Blake.
4. "We have a copy in our school library," added Freddie.
5. fail, succeed: antonym

WEEK 3: ACTIVITY 4

1. Noun
2. Verb
3. Jack said, "We have never been hiking down that trail."
4. "Bring that compass or we will get lost," suggested Gerry.
5. sale, sail; Sentences will vary.

WEEK 3: ACTIVITY 5

1. Capitalization error
2. No mistake
3. Spelling error
4. Punctuation error
5. Punctuation error

BONUS ACTIVITY: FACT OR OPINION

1. Opinion   2. Fact   3. Opinion   4. Fact
5. Opinion

WEEK 4: ACTIVITY 1

1. "Where are we going on our class trip?" asked Ricky.
2. "How about the Royal Ontario Museum?" suggested Mr. Cummings.
3. Halifax: proper noun
4. hockey, baseball
5. Kingston, Brandon

WEEK 4: ACTIVITY 2

1. eye, I; Sentences will vary.
2. shelf: shelves
3. woman: women
4. Sarah and Becky brought juice boxes to the class party.
5. Let's join that game of soccer with those boys.

WEEK 4: ACTIVITY 3

1. Car, airplane
2. Hockey game
3. Polly's favourite place to eat is Golden Grill on Main Street.
4. They serve the best burgers and fries in the whole town.
5. caribou   moose   (zebra)   elk   reindeer

WEEK 4: ACTIVITY 4

1. wol – ver – ine
2. Ed – mon – ton
3. A totem is an animal or object that is a symbol of a family or tribe.
4. When the symbols are carved on logs, they make a totem pole.
5. Dr.

WEEK 4: ACTIVITY 5

1. The howling wind blew the snow into high drifts.
2. The water is cold but the sun is warm.
3. My friend is coming over and we are going to see a movie.
4. When our team won the trophy, our picture was in the newspaper.
5. My brother's alarm is so noisy it wakes me up every day.

SSR1146   ISBN: 9781771587327 © On The Mark Press

Bonus Activity: Right on Track!

1. tiny   2. easy   3. brave   4. timid   5. happy
6. clever

Week 5: Activity 1

1. cookies: plural
2. Carol asked, "Who spilled my milk all over my desk?"
3. Laura, Carol's friend, had seen who made the mess.
4. What time is it? Question
5. I will give you a ride to school. Statement

Week 5: Activity 2

1. Fact
2. Fantasy
3. Give me your phone number and I will call you tonight.
4. Harry and Sam are working on that project together.
5. going to summer camp; Answers will vary.

Week 5: Activity 3

1. good   better   best
2. sunny   sunnier   sunniest
3. We stayed indoors for recess because it was raining hard outside.
4. If I give you ten dimes, will you give me a loonie?
5. There was a gold ring sitting on the window sill by the sink.

Week 5: Activity 4

1. tree branches apple leaves twig
2. How much money do you have in your pocket?
3. "Don't leave you bike in the driveway," said my dad.
4. moon is to night as sun is to: day
5. whale is to huge as ant is to: tiny

Week 5: Activity 5

1. We are going to Sudbury to visit our grandparents.
2. We need to buy a ticket to go on the train.
3. The person at the service desk sold us the right ticket.
4. We were waiting to get on our train.
5. Our parents waved goodbye to us from the platform.

Bonus Activity: Holiday Eating

1. This restaurant is advertising for the holiday of Thanksgiving.
2. The most expensive meal is Seafood Special.
3. The restaurant is open for 10 hours on Sunday and Monday.

Week 6: Activity 1

1. This summer we are going to Kids Camp on Whitefish Lake.
2. Everyone will be able to go canoeing, swimming, fishing, and hiking.
3. potato: potatoes
4. daisy: daisies
5. Stayed in the air

Week 6: Activity 2

1. Suggestions: due, new, flew, moo, too
2. Doing the laundry
3. Flying a kite
4. You will need to listen so you will know how to do your work.
5. "Did Ned sprain his ankle in the football game?" asked Victor.

Week 6: Activity 3

1. A person who cuts down trees
2. The old truck chugged along the dusty road.
3. The rabbit nibbled at the carrots and the lettuce.
4. "Have you read the poem Indian Summer?" asked Miss Thatcher.
5. "We will study pioneer life this year," said Mr. Collins.

Week 6: Activity 4

1. The magician's tricks were the best I have ever seen.
2. He asked people from the audience to help him with some tricks.
3. Not a sentence
4. Sentence
5. gentle, rough; Sentences will vary.

Week 6: Activity 5

1. Does Mom plan to take us shopping for new shoes?
2. I will help her with her homework if she asks me.
3. The best part of this movie is coming right up.

4. Here <u>comes</u> Willy now. He was almost late.
5. Grandpa <u>was</u> building a surprise in his workshop.

BONUS ACTIVITY: ANALOGIES

1. Pencil is to write as brush is to paint.
2. Cow is to milk as chicken is to egg.
3. Crayons are to colour as scissors are to cut.
4. Skating is to winter as swimming is to summer.
5. Cat is to kitten as dog is to puppy.
6. Foot is to leg as hand is to arm.

WEEK 7: ACTIVITY 1

1. It was time for the bus to come so I got my jacket.
2. The leaves turned red, yellow, and orange.
3. Their (new) puppy has (short), (fluffy) (brown) fur.
4. Ice cream is a (sweet) and (cold) treat.
5. Opinion

WEEK 7: ACTIVITY 2

1. man: men
2. baby: babies
3. damp, dry; Sentence will vary.
4. Farmer Brown has cows, horses, and pigs on his farm.
5. We studied how to spell the names of Canada's provinces.

WEEK 7: ACTIVITY 3

1. intelligent: smart, clever, bright
2. My sister and I sold our old toys at our yard sale.
3. There is ice and snow at the top of that mountain.
4. In a parade
5. At the library

WEEK 7: ACTIVITY 4

1. "What would you like for lunch?" asked Mom.
2. "How about chicken noodle soup?" I answered.
3. lunch (breakfast) (dinner) snack (supper)
4. my brother's wagon
5. Sally's red hat

WEEK 7: ACTIVITY 5

1. dictionary
2. cookbook
3. telephone book
4. encyclopedia
5. thesaurus, dictionary

BONUS ACTIVITY: WHICH WORD DOESN'T BELONG?

1. sky
2. moss
3. happy
4. ever
5. lightning
6. brown

WEEK 8: ACTIVITY 1

1. Many totem poles can be seen in British Columbia.
2. We went there on our summer vacation last July.
3. doesn't: does not
4. I'm: I am
5. Canada's Wonderland: proper noun

WEEK 8: ACTIVITY 2

1. eye is to look as ear is to hear
2. chair is to sit as bed is to lie (down)
3. library
4. It's your turn to help with dishes tonight, Anna.
5. I think your flashlight is brighter than mine.

WEEK 8: ACTIVITY 3

1. Winnipeg: city
2. Edmonton Oilers: hockey team
3. Can you sing *O' Canada* in English and French?
4. My favourite TV show, <u>Kids Speak Out</u>, is on each Thursday.
5. Interrogative

WEEK 8: ACTIVITY 4

1. We were cheering and clapping for the home team.
2. "What street do you live on?" asked Jerry's mom.
3. <u>That's</u> the best game I have ever played!
4. 2-lightning, 1-lace, 3-lodge
5. 1-desert, 2-detail, 3-devil

WEEK 8: ACTIVITY 5

1. Jessie is the fastest runner so he easily won the race.
2. Those cookies are hot because Mom just took them out of the oven.
3. Hector was late getting to the bus stop so he missed the bus to school.
4. If you come to my house on Saturday, we can play in my tree house.
5. Our class is going on a trip to the planetarium.

SSR1146   ISBN: 9781771587327 © On The Mark Press

Bonus Activity: Suffix Word Search

t		n							
	h	e	n	d	l	e	s	s	
b	e	a	u	t	i	f	u	l	
	l		t	n					y
	p	l	k						l
	f	y	l	e	f	a	s		t
	u					u			f
	l	o	u	d	l	y	l		o
c	a	r	e	f	u	l			s
	s	s	e	l	e	c	i	r	p

Week 9: Activity 1

1. Past
2. Future
3. The bear caught a fish in its paw and ate it.
4. "What is our math homework for tonight?" asked Peter.
5. sugar

Week 9: Activity 2

1. read: reread
2. like: dislike
3. Fact
4. I have a cat named Ginger and a fish named Goldie.
5. Rory wants to play on our school soccer team next year.

Week 9: Activity 3

1. Opening, greeting
2. Mom's job is at the Queenston General Hospital in Surrey.
3. We saw a double rainbow in the sky yesterday.
4. restaurant: 3
5. Saskatchewan: 4

Week 9: Activity 4

1. Willy and I read a good story called The Treasure of Hidden Bay.
2. It was an adventure story about two friends looking for a lost chest.
3. A sweet food served at the end of a meal.
4. In a classroom
5. At a birthday party

Week 9: Activity 5

1. Capitalization error
2. No mistake
3. Spelling error
4. Capitalization error
5. Punctuation error

Bonus Activity: Terrific Titles!

Answers will vary.
1. a cookbook for making foods for kids' lunches
2. a TV show about living in Canada's North.
3. a movie about being lost overnight in a thick forest
4. a book telling how to be a successful birdwatcher
5. a book about the life story of a sports hero

Week 10: Activity 1

1. heard
2. aanswer
3. I set my alarm clock for 6:00 a.m. which is early for me
4. Grandma asked, "Will you help me weed the garden?"
5. Father is to man as mother is to woman.

Week 10: Activity 2

1. print: reprinted, unprintable
2. appear: disappearance, disappeared
3. Opinion
4. I like reading mystery stories about life on the sea.
5. My favourite book is Monsters of the Deep by J. J. Dunn.

Week 10: Activity 3

1. 3-neon, 2-nasty, 4-nimble, 1-napkin
2. My very best friends are Ginny, Kara, and Adele.
3. Those big boys were teasing the little boys on the playground.
4. tiny, tinier, tiniest
5. beautiful, more beautiful, most beautiful

Week 10: Activity 4

1. We had maple syrup cotton candy at Gibbons Family Farm.
2. "Will your business trip last long?" I asked Dad.
3. please: ease, tease, squeeze, breeze
4. Kelowna: 3
5. Edmundston: 3

WEEK 10: ACTIVITY 5

1. When the pitcher threw the ball, I hit it and got a home run!
2. Daffodils are pretty yellow flowers that grow in the spring.
3. Our new puppy chews everything, including my new shoes, which made Mom mad.
4. I have such a bad cold that I need to stay in bed and miss school.
5. My aunt, who lives in Calgary, is visiting for two weeks.

BONUS ACTIVITY: SAME OR OPPOSITE?

yellow	orange	orange	yellow
orange	orange	yellow	orange
yellow	yellow	orange	yellow

WEEK 11: ACTIVITY 1

1. My dentist, Dr. Forrester, told me to brush my teeth more carefully.
2. We heard the sound of footsteps coming down the hallway.
3. Future
4. Past
5. (beat) bread (sea) (realize) thread

WEEK 11: ACTIVITY 2

1. Not a sentence
2. Sentence
3. "Are you ready for the math quiz on Tuesday?" asked Dan.
4. "I have studied my number facts for hours," I replied.
5. enjoyable: joy

WEEK 11: ACTIVITY 3

1. The track at Westwood High School is a great place to run.
2. Carl and I like to go there after school for a few hours.
3. Superior Erie (Atlantic) Huron Ontario
4. maple elm oak spruce (palm)
5. plumber

WEEK 11: ACTIVITY 4

1. Fact

2. Fiction
3. Last Saturday, our family took a hike to Rock Dunder.
4. At the top, we sat at a table and ate our lunch.
5. (shoe) (blue) doe (grew) sew

WEEK 11: ACTIVITY 5

1. My brother and I went to Green Valley Camp last summer.
2. Of all the activities we did, we liked swimming the best.
3. At night, we sat around a big campfire.
4. We heard some scary stories from the leaders.
5. We also got to toast marshmallows and make S'mores.

BONUS ACTIVITY: MAKING COMPOUND WORDS

1. rainbow
2. sunshine
3. houseboat
4. soapsuds
5. pancake

WEEK 12: ACTIVITY 1

1. The horse could run like the wind. Run very fast
2. We bought pencils, crayons, and markers at Sam's Supersave.
3. The squirrel ran to the top of the tree in Maggie's yard.
4. We
5. She

WEEK 12: ACTIVITY 2

1. We saw a rainbow after the rain had stopped.
2. My favourite colours are purple, blue, and green.
3. great: greater, greatest
4. funny: funnier, funniest
5. Opinion

WEEK 12: ACTIVITY 3

1. "Give me back my soccer ball!" screamed Nancy.
2. We are going to go to see the new Disney movie on Saturday.
3. baseball
4. pumpkin
5. Common noun

SSR1146 ISBN: 9781771587327 © On The Mark Press

Week 12: Activity 4

1. Kenny rides his bike too fast down that street.
2. The kitten washed its face with its little paw.
3. 1946 Brandon Drive: Address
4. Body
5. Which one / What kind

Week 12: Activity 5

1. Capitalization
2. Spelling
3. Spelling
4. No mistake
5. Punctuation

Bonus Activity: Dictionary
                      Detectives

YES   1. Can a yak bite you?
YES   2. Is cement heavy?
NO   3. Is an aileron found on a tractor?
NO   4. Does grotesque mean the same as beautiful?
NO   5. Does a quintet have six people?

Week 13: Activity 1

1. would not: wouldn't
2. Excuse me, Sandy, what time is it right now?
3. Wow! That was a very close race to the finish.
4. He
5. Them

Week 13: Activity 2

1. Willy is to William as Joey is to: Joseph
2. Sandy is to Sandra as Susie is to: Susan
3. Larry, please turn those lights off.
4. Last Friday, we went shopping at the Westgate Mall.
5. write, right; Sentences will vary.

Week 13: Activity 3

1. 5-paste, 1-package, 4-partner, 2-palace, 3-paper
2. Have you read the story called Princess Scarface?
3. Many fairy tales have an evil witch and a good witch.
4. crown: brown, down, clown, frown, town
5. nine: dine, fine, line, mine, pine, wine, whine, vine

Week 13: Activity 4

1. Sept.
2. Remember to bring rubber boots for our hike to Martin's Marsh.
3. If the weather is good, we will have a picnic there.
4. unlikely: like
5. happiness: happy

Week 13: Activity 5

1. encyclopedia
2. dictionary
3. encyclopedia
4. telephone book
5. thesaurus

Bonus Activity: Categories

1. Things on a Bed
2. Wild Animals
3. Things with Wheels
4. Food for Lunch
5. Things Used for Writing

Week 14: Activity 1

1. What do you do in your spare time for fun?
2. I like reading, drawing, and playing soccer with my friends.
3. Bonavista: 4
4. Toronto Blue Jays: team
5. Big Ben: horse

Week 14: Activity 2

1. My sister is going be a nurse when she grows up.
2. I want to be a scientist who travels to Canada's North.
3. grand: and, band, bland, brand, grand, land, sand,
4. down: clown, frown, drown, town, brown,
5. Things used in building

Week 14: Activity 3

1. they've: they have
2. I'd: I should, I would
3. "Who is the author of The Cat in the Hat?" asked Tracey.
4. "I'm not going get any needle today!" screamed Polly.
5. battle, fight: synonyms

Week 14: Activity 4

1. I am going to ask Henry, Jamie, and Zeke to play basketball.
2. We have some secret plays we would like to try on the other team.
3. She
4. It
5. A cure; something that heals or prevents

Week 14: Activity 5

1. The principal (spoke) to us yesterday.
2. The ice has (frozen) on our pond.
3. I will try to (find) your lost mittens.
4. Wally (chose) to stay at home today.
5. Our school bell (rings) at the same time each morning.

Bonus Activity: Name Those Nouns

blue			blue	blue
	blue	blue		
blue			blue	blue

Week 15: Activity 1

1. She
2. It
3. Nov.
4. On rainy days, we like to sit and read a book.
5. "Which baseball team is your favourite?" asked Ben.

Week 15: Activity 2

1. Not a sentence
2. The Atlantic Ocean can be dangerous when its windy.
3. Fishermen have a hard life on rough seas.
4. puppy: puppies
5. church: churches

Week 15: Activity 3

1. Charlottetown: 3
2. (He) will take (me) with (him) to the beach.
3. (She) likes (it) so much (she) will keep (it).
4. "We are going to Canada's Wonderland this August," said Jenny.
5. "Do you have a favourite ride?" I asked.

Week 15: Activity 4

1. Past
2. Future
3. "Do you think third grade is hard?" asked Helen.
4. "We'll have to listen and work hard," answered Mya.
5. feather: leather, weather

Week 15: Activity 5

1. A skunk has black fur <u>and</u> a white stripe on its back and tail.
2. It is not dangerous <u>but</u> you should stay away from one.
3. Skunks sleep during the day <u>and</u> they hunt at night.
4. If you startle it <u>and</u> scare it, it may spray you.
5. A skunk has short legs <u>but</u> it can move quickly.

Bonus Activity: Where's the Action?

yellow	yellow			yellow
yellow				
	yellow	yellow		yellow

Week 16: Activity 1

1. Soccer game
2. Noun
3. Verb
4. Have you ever read the book called <u>Haunted Canada</u>?
5. It has some of the scariest stories I have read.

Week 16: Activity 2

1. Fact
2. went: bent, dent, lent, meant, vent
3. dawn: fawn, lawn, pawn, Shawn, gone
4. Each province in Canada has its own flag and flower.
5. "Do you know which street Della lives on?" asked Rick.

Week 16: Activity 3

1. mountainous: moun – tain – ous
2. overboard: o – ver – board
3. call: caller, calls, called, calling
4. "What time does the movie begin?" asked Tyler.

SSR1146   ISBN: 9781771587327 © On The Mark Press

5. "Do you mean <u>Adventures of the Lost World</u>?" replied Jane.

WEEK 14: ACTIVITY 4

1. She knew that she was going be in trouble.
2. I broke my mom's best dish yesterday.
3. tractor: common
4. Robert Munsch: proper
5. leaves: leaf

WEEK 16: ACTIVITY 5

1. Apples, bananas, and oranges are fruits.
2. Cows, horses, and chickens live on a farm.
3. Tomatoes and green beans grow in the garden.
4. You can see ocean for miles and sometimes you see an ocean liner.
5. Canada's north is a cold, harsh place so very few people live there.

BONUS ACTIVITY: CANADA BIRDS WORD SEARCH

c	a	r	d	i	n	a	l			r
h						l				o
n	i	f	f	u	p		o			b
	c							o		i
	k			s	w	a	n			n
b	l	u	e	j	a	y				
				d						
	c	r	o	w		n	e	r	w	
							e			
c	a	n	a	d	a	g	o	o	s	e

WEEK 17: ACTIVITY 1

1. Please give me that soccer ball so we can play a game.
2. We saw the Prime Minister in Ottawa last July.
3. overdoing: do
4. trickster: trick
5. thought (tough) though (rough) cough

WEEK 17: ACTIVITY 2

1. Which one
2. My baby brother, Lewis, will be one on April 10, 2016.
3. He wants chocolate cupcakes instead of a birthday cake.
4. ways to move

WEEK 17: ACTIVITY 3

1. Adjective
2. Noun
3. friend
4. We have to buy apples, cookies, and juice boxes.
5. Marianne is going to be late for her lesson.

WEEK 17: ACTIVITY 4

1. Fact
2. Opinion
3. Joey doesn't want to go to bed early tonight.
4. We listened to the story <u>Lighthouse in the Fog</u>.
5. bent: curved, crooked   safe: unharmed, secure, unhurt

WEEK 17: ACTIVITY 5

1. Yesterday I lost my new jacket on the bus.
2. We hiked along the trail for three hours and then we stopped for lunch.
3. Would you like a hot dog with mustard and ketchup on it?
4. I think my brother took my cookies because I see a trail of crumbs.
5. Because there are dark clouds in the sky, I think a storm will begin soon.

BONUS ACTIVITY: IDIOMS

1. not understood
2. very happy or excited
3. be quiet; stop talking
4. tell a secret
5. sound asleep

WEEK 18: ACTIVITY 1

1. synonyms
2. antonyms
3. Our team lost the final game against the Rockwood Raiders.
4. I wants chocolate syrup, sprinkles, and peanuts on my sundae.
5. Verb

WEEK 18: ACTIVITY 2

1. The newest style of clothes, trends

2. Weird, unusual
3. "Can you tell me where to hang this picture?" asked Uncle Jim.
4. My sister and I will walk to Carrie's house on Pineview Street.
5. not a sentence

WEEK 18: ACTIVITY 3

1. Gabby said, "I think you should finish your work now."
2. We listened to the song Home again on the radio.
3. Prefix
4. Suffix
5. Your cousin, Piper: Closing

WEEK 18: ACTIVITY 4

1. 3-fish   2-fight   5-fixture   1-field   4-five
2. "I can't find my keys anywhere," said Mom.
3. "I think I saw them on the table in the hall," I offered.
4. In the garden, flowerbeds
5. Skating show or competition

WEEK 18: ACTIVITY 5

1. Listen to this adventure story.
2. Did you hear the fans cheering for him?
3. This music is too loud for me.
4. They're going to come here for a visit.
5. There is their new car.

BONUS ACTIVITY: ANALOGIES

1. sock
2. bed
3. beach
4. sun
5. black

WEEK 19: ACTIVITY 1:

1. Did you hear your sister calling you to dinner?
2. School starts at 9:15 AM sharp each day.
3. Taking a bath
4. soft: hard, rough, loud
5. sunny: cloudy, dull

WEEK 19: ACTIVITY 2

1. rules but amuse value funny human
2. The picture on that postcard is beautiful.
3. We gave Mom some flowers for Mother's Day.
4. Past
5. Future

WEEK 19: ACTIVITY 3

1. 2-blast   3-bleak   1-black   5-blind   4-blend
2. Subject
3. Predicate
4. I left my new jacket at the Playview Park last Saturday.
5. We saw a rainbow after the storm on Thursday.

WEEK 19: ACTIVITY 4

1. Parent / Grandparent
2. Teacher
3. thief
4. Which movie did you like best, Frozen or Zootopia?
5. We collected eggs at Uncle Harry's farm last Sunday.

WEEK 19: ACTIVITY 5

1. birth day
2. after noon
3. class room
4. down stairs
5. skate board

BONUS ACTIVITY: LISTEN TO THE SOUND

1. The wind howls .
2. Bacon sizzles.
3. Fire crackles .
4. The telephone rings.
5. Thunder rumbles.
6. The train whistles.

WEEK 20: ACTIVITY 1

1. Giant is to tall as elf is to short.
2. round: around, bound, mound, pound, sound
3. cold: bold, fold, gold, mould, sold,
4. Our family has gone to Cape Spear in Newfoundland.
5. You can see the city of St. John's and the harbour.

SSR1146   ISBN: 9781771587327 © On The Mark Press

WEEK 20: ACTIVITY 2

1. We are going to order pizza from Pizza Plus on Friday night.
2. For dessert we will have ice cream sandwiches.
3. dictionary: 4
4. imagination: 5
5. Calgary Flames: hockey team

WEEK 20: ACTIVITY 3

1. RCMP
2. "Don't forget to pick up your toys," called Mom.
3. We have lived in Cornwall, Ontario for two years.
4. doesn't: does not
5. he'll: he will; he shall

WEEK 20: ACTIVITY 4

1. unpainted: paint
2. hopelessly: hope
3. We went for a picnic in Woodland Park on Sunday.
4. Some ants crawled onto the table and headed for the food.
5. crayons   markers   (erasers)   coloured   pencils

WEEK 20: ACTIVITY 5

1. Rob and I are going to play on the soccer team.
2. Some of our friends are going to join him and me.
3. Rob and I had a great time!
4. The coach showed him and me some good moves.
5. Rob and I were proud of what we had learned.

BONUS ACTIVITY: DICTIONARY DETECTIVES

1. smell
2. two
3. grasp
4. get bigger
5. not cooked
6. run

WEEK 21: ACTIVITY 1

1. Selena's new puppy
2. my dad's truck
3. "What colour is your favourite?" asked Pete.
4. "Definitely, I like red the best," I replied.
5. moist

WEEK 21: ACTIVITY 2

1. Because it is snowing, our bus will arrive late for school.
2. The bell rings at 9:10 a.m. sharp every morning.
3. loud: cloud, proud, crowd
4. gift: lift, sift, drift
5. Schoolyard

WEEK 21: ACTIVITY 3

1. chipmunk
2. We are doing a play called The Lonely Christmas Tree for our parents.
3. Our teacher, Miss Drake, is bringing a huge tree for us.
4. Fantasy
5. Fact

WEEK 21: ACTIVITY 4

1. We are reading a book called Ramona the Pest in our class.
2. Some people like the story, but others don't.
3. stomach   k
4. chocolate   ch
5. cloudy: sunny

WEEK 21: ACTIVITY 5

1. cookbook
2. dictionary
3. encyclopedia
4. telephone book
5. thesaurus

BONUS ACTIVITY: CANADIAN CRITTERS

1. seal
2. skunk
3. rabbit
4. raccoon
5. squirrel

WEEK 22: ACTIVITY 1

1. Opinion
2. Fact
3. infant   incorrect   include   (inch)   insect
4. Hallie has broken all her new crayons and pencils.
5. We don't have enough time to finish our work before lunch.

Week 22: Activity 2

1. thunderstorm: 3
2. They
3. he
4. Have you ever read the magazine called <u>Just for Kids</u>?
5. It has a lot of good information, jokes, and puzzles.

Week 22: Activity 3

1. Antlers are to deer as tusks are to: elephants
2. Milk is to cow as egg is to: chicken
3. toast
4. Someone left the light on all night in the kitchen
5. I likes to play the game, Apples, with my friends.

Week 22: Activity 4

1. Police officer
2. "Who is in charge of this job?" asked Mr. Miller.
3. We took many pictures when we were at Niagara Falls, Ontario.
4. Angry, very upset
5. People

Week 22: Activity 5

1. I love to swim at the beach on hot days.
2. My friend, Gary, is coming over to play video games.
3. I am having a birthday party on Saturday.
4. The parade we watched had clowns doing tricks and a marching band.
5. My kitten, Poppy, washes her face using her paws.

Bonus Activity: What's the Time?

1. Past
2. Present / Future
3. Past
4. Future / Present
5. Past

Week 23: Activity 1

1. "I'm grumpy. I need a nap," said Grandpa
2. "Would you like me to make you a cup of tea?" I asked.
3. An unsteady light
4. hilly   hint   hide   (hiccup)   hitch
5. radish   railway   (raccoon)   rather   rascal

Week 23: Activity 2

1. Because it was rainy outside, we didn't play in the yard.
2. "That's a great pair of soccer cleats," said Coach Brock.
3. Future
4. Past
5. does not: doesn't

Week 23: Activity 3

1. This salad has lettuce, cucumbers, and tomatoes in it.
2. Pedro is training his dog to do two new tricks.
3. defend, protect: synonyms
4. Opinion
5. Fact

Week 23: Activity 4

1. Dear Aunt Hilda; greeting /opening
2. back: pack   black   quack   flack   smack
3. trick: Dick   Rick   flick   quick   sick
4. Doesn't he have two brothers and one sister?
5. Jillian and I want to go to see that movie <u>Monsterville</u>.

Week 23: Activity 5

1. Spelling error
2. Capitalization error
3. Punctuation
4. Capitalization
5. No mistake

Bonus Activity: Baby Animals

	f	a	w	n		p	u	p
	o					i		
c	a	l	f			g		k
	l	a	m	b		l		i
						e		d
						t		

Week 24: Activity 1

1. Playful
2. This Christmas we are going to Aunt Jan's house in Edmonton.
3. Will you teach me how to skip Double Dutch?

SSR1146   ISBN: 9781771587327 © On The Mark Press

4. snake is to hiss as duck is to: quack
5. hot is to fire as cold is to: ice

WEEK 24: ACTIVITY 2

1. stop: stops, stopped, stopping, stopper
2. cry: cries, crying, cried, crier
3. My family and I are going to our cottage on Red Lake.
4. We go fishing swimming and hiking all the time.
5. question

WEEK 24: ACTIVITY 3

1. My brother and I are getting new bikes this summer.
2. The Grade 3 class performed a play called The Friendly Dragon.
3. Everyone clapped and cheered when the dragon saved the little boy.
4. His
5. It

WEEK 24: ACTIVITY 4

1. "How did this plate get broken?" asked Mom.
2. Jenny brought her markers, pencils, and crayons to school.
3. mister: Mr.
4. December: Dec.
5. Adjective

WEEK 24: ACTIVITY 5

1. Aren't these flowers beautiful? I
2. The ants are invading our picnic! E
3. Quick, move the food and the plates. C
4. It is very peaceful in the park. S
5. Would you like to stay here longer? I

BONUS ACTIVITY: AWESOME ADVERBS!

softly	trains	easily	there
snow	early	here	circus
house	quietly	bird	later

WEEK 25: ACTIVITY 1

1. Do you like chicken noodle soup and crackers?
2. I eat it for lunch every Saturday because Mom makes it.

3. the books of the teacher: the teacher's books
4. the pencils of the students: the students' pencils
5. isn't: is not

WEEK 25: ACTIVITY 2

1. Max and I want to help Simon wash his bike on Saturday.
2. Simon is riding his bike in the parade.
3. Question
4. Marystown: 3
5. Shediac: 3

WEEK 25: ACTIVITY 3

1. Noun
2. Verb
3. Let's meet at the playground at 6:30 p.m. to play soccer.
4. Bring your friends, Monty and Devon to play too.
5. 5-navy, 2-napkin, 3-nation, 4-nature, 1-nag

WEEK 25: ACTIVITY 4

1. Will you ask Ms Wilson to help us with this question?
2. How much money do you have in your piggy bank?
3. What kind
4. Opinion
5. Fact

WEEK 25: ACTIVITY 5

1. We are taking our puppy to Dr. Willows our vet.
2. Having a toad in your garden is a good thing.
3. Who knew the most answers to the math quiz?
4. When is Tim's library book due?
5. They're moving to a new apartment soon.

BONUS ACTIVITY: SMALLEST? BIGGEST?

1. bicycle/ airplane / bus/ car/ roller skates / train
2. cup/ bowl/ plate/ glass/ platter / spoon
3. bracelet/ crown / ring / watch/ necklace
4. teenager/ baby / parent / toddler/ Grade 3 student
5. body / finger/ arm/ leg/ head/ foot
6. toonie/ quarter/ dime / loonie/ $5 bill

WEEK 26: ACTIVITY 1

1. Past
2. Future

3. Did you remember to pack your bathing suit, goggles and swim fins?
4. I am so excited to be going to Sandbanks Provincial Park on Saturday.
5. B is to letter as 9 is to: number

WEEK 26: ACTIVITY 2

1. king, queen: antonyms
2. ruin, wreck: synonyms
3. furniture: fur – ni – ture
4. An earthquake hit Japan and caused a lot of damage.
5. I hope I get to go with Dad to the Riverview Annual Boat Show.

WEEK 26: ACTIVITY 3

1. We
2. He
3. Our class is going to the Royal Canadian Mint in Ottawa.
4. Have you ever been to the top of the CN Tower?
5. carry: carried

WEEK 26: ACTIVITY 4

1. "Will you trade four quarters for a loonie?" asked Ethan.
2. We eat our lunch at 11:40 a.m. each day at school.
3. Verb
4. Adverb
5. hair, hare: Sentences will vary

WEEK 26: ACTIVITY 5

1. thesaurus
2. encyclopedia
3. telephone book
4. dictionary
5. cookbook

BONUS ACTIVITY: WHAT SHALL I WEAR?

1. safety boots
2. a fancy dress
3. a fireproof suit
4. a white coat and hat
5. a camouflage suit
6. a dark uniform

WEEK 27: ACTIVITY 1

1. "Wes, you're a great runner!" exclaimed Troy.
2. I hope it doesn't rain on Sunday and spoil our picnic.
3. shouldn't: should not
4. he's: he is
5. powder   poke   polish   (polecat)   pout

WEEK 27: ACTIVITY 2

1. tooth: teeth
2. box: boxes
3. Geraldton: 3
4. I needs to shop for rain boots before spring gets here.
5. Aunt Rose has gone to see Dr. Martins because she feels sick.

WEEK 27: ACTIVITY 3

1. Correct; no mistakes
2. That hail storm will devastate our crop of wheat. Totally destroy or ruin
3. "My favourite puppy is the all black one," said Casey.
4. "Maybe you could name it Snowball," I joked.
5. How many

WEEK 27: ACTIVITY 4

1. head: dead, dread, bread, lead, fed, red, said
2. Canada is a part of the continent of North America.
3. Hector is going to be late if he doesn't hurry up.
4. My sister likes (strawberries), (blueberries) and (raspberries).
5. The pet shop sells (birds), (gerbils) and (hamsters).

WEEK 27: ACTIVITY 5

1. (mr) and (mrs) (campbell) moved to (kitchener).
2. (did) (ben) take a picture of that huge maple tree?
3. (charlotte) won the first prize for drawing .
4. (oh), (david), what a mess you have made !
5. (who) is going with you to Oshawa on (saturday)?

SSR1146   ISBN: 9781771587327 © On The Mark Press

BONUS ACTIVITY: IN MY CLASSROOM, YOU WILL FIND ...

		c	s	k	o	o	b		c
	g	h						h	
b	l	a	c	k	b	o	a	r	d
	u	i				l	p		e
	e	r		k		e			s
		c	r	a	y	o	n	s	k
r	e	t	u	p	m	o	c		
r	u	l	e	r	t	n	i	a	p
r	e	h	c	a	e	t	l		
s	c	i	s	s	o	r	s		

WEEK 28: ACTIVITY 1

1. (I am wearing my mittens) because it is cold out today.
2. If you waste time, (you will be late).
3. Terry has broken another window with his football.
4. My cousin, Kelly, has a new baby girl named Quinn.
5. Adele <u>told</u> us she would help us with our math. tell

WEEK 28: ACTIVITY 2

1. Fast food drive thru window.
2. Do you think you will be able to go with us on Friday?
3. We watched The Land That Time Forgot last night on TV.
4. Opinion
5. Fact

WEEK 28: ACTIVITY 3

1. Subject
2. Predicate
3. Future
4. In math, we add, subtract, multiply, and divide.
5. Mother cat takes good care of her babies and keeps them safe.

WEEK 28: ACTIVITY 4

1. radio is to listen as television is to: watch
2. You're not looking at the right page in your book.
3. My dad likes most sports but he likes golf the best.
4. The car drove (quickly) and (carelessly) down our street.
5. The fans cheered (loudly) for the home team.

WEEK 28: ACTIVITY 5

1. Spelling error
2. punctuation error
3. No mistake
4. capitalization error
5. punctuation error

BONUS ACTIVITY: WHAT GROWS IN MY GARDEN?

1. potatoes
2. carrot
3. peas
4. beet
5. tomatoes
6. cucumber

WEEK 29: ACTIVITY 1

1. Elise and I don't have any reading homework tonight.
2. Kenny has a new job at the Supersuds Car Wash.
3. feet: plural
4. dragons: plural
5. Command

WEEK 29: ACTIVITY 2

1. "Reagan, why weren't you at school yesterday?" asked Pam.
2. The red car came speeding down Brock Street.
3. live
4. Expensive glassware
5. hear: heard

WEEK 29: ACTIVITY 3

1. Those chattering squirrels like to run high in our trees.
2. I won't be in the race tomorrow because I hurt my ankle.
3. Bay of Fundy: proper noun
4. shipwreck: common noun
5. blue, yellow

SSR1146   ISBN: 9781771587327 © On The Mark Press

WEEK 29: ACTIVITY 4

1. farthest: far
2. hopping: hop
3. Sadie and I are going to the grocery store to get pizza dough.
4. We also need pepperoni, cheese, and tomato sauce.
5. familiar : fa – mil - iar

WEEK 29: ACTIVITY 5

1. We went to the petting zoo and fed the animals.
2. The dandelion seeds floated away because it was very windy.
3. Lizards are reptiles that are cold-blooded.
4. You should be proud of your great science project.
5. You can build a castle or a wall in the sand.

BONUS ACTIVITY: CANADA BIRDS UNSCRAMBLE

1. blue jay
2. chickadee
3. robin
4. seagull
5. swallow
6. cardinal
7. pigeon
8. puffin

WEEK 30: ACTIVITY 1

1. Fiction
2. Riding the roller coaster is fun, isn't it?
3. Canadians celebrate Thanksgiving Day in October.
4. ocean
5. yellow

WEEK 30: ACTIVITY 2

1. sob, weep: synonyms
2. Freddie and I have done all the dishes.
3. Jed has eaten his sandwich and drank his milk.
4. information: 4
5. assembly: 3

WEEK 30: ACTIVITY 3

1. Are we going to go fishing on Saturday, Grandpa?
2. Those crickets were chirping loudly all night.
3. reheated: heat
4. 2-flap   3-flare   4-flash   1-flag
5. 2-orbit   4-ore   1-orange   3-order

WEEK 30: ACTIVITY 4

1. Who wrote the book The Mouse and the Motorcycle?
2. We walk our dog, Rico, every night after dinner.
3. future
4. We visited our grandmother in Hamilton.
5. Jenny and her sister help their neighbour every Saturday.

WEEK 30: ACTIVITY 5

1. The bus has arrived on time.
2. Karlee and I are going shopping at the new mall.
3. You did much better work this time.
4. Sue has bought a new umbrella.
5. We saw a double rainbow in the sky.

BONUS ACTIVITY: YUM!!

Two Syllable: poutine, French toast, apples
Three Syllable: beaver tails, mac and cheese
Four Syllable: maple syrup

WEEK 31: ACTIVITY 1

1. really
2. friend
3. It was an accident when I broke the old dish.
4. Kim lives at the corner of Queen and Elm Streets.
5. said: say

WEEK 31: ACTIVITY 2

1. What kind / which one
2. How many
3. Donnie doesn't like any vegetables but corn.
4. Julie asked, "What time are we leaving today?"
5. The bell rang (so we lined up).

WEEK 31: ACTIVITY 3

1. names of planets
2. names of numbers
3. Future
4. I like the story Clifford the Big Red Dog.
5. Who sings that song playing on the radio?

SSR1146   ISBN: 9781771587327 © On The Mark Press

WEEK 31: ACTIVITY 4

1. When
2. Do you believe that story about the tigers?
3. "Do you like rainy or sunny weather?" asked Fanny.
4. Not a sentence
5. Sentence

WEEK 31: ACTIVITY 5

1. He's
2. I'll
3. isn't
4. There's
5. Let's

BONUS ACTIVITY: CATEGORIES

Answers will vary.

WEEK 32: ACTIVITY 1

1. Do you know the way to the nearest hardware store?
2. We have ordered a large pizza from Pizza Palace.
3. crow (cow) grown (frown)
4. beautiful: pretty, attractive
5. completed: finished, done

WEEK 32: ACTIVITY 2

1. Airport
2. Our dog, Spike, chewed my new shoes.
3. Grandma's making me a new blue dress.
4. Dad hammered the boards into place.
5. The old log cabin was Great Grandpa's first home.

WEEK 32: ACTIVITY 3

1. Not a sentence
2. Sentence
3. "Don't be late for the game," called Coach Jones.
4. Our team wears blue and red shirts for each game.
5. wing is to bird as fin is to: fish

WEEK 32: ACTIVITY 4

1. Rachel and Ashley will sing a duet at the concert.
2. I won't ever touch those thistles again! (or end with a period.)
3. You and I are going to have a great time! (or end with a period.)
4. breeze: freeze, sneeze, squeeze, please
5. cross: boss, floss, loss, moss

WEEK 32: ACTIVITY 5

board: 2
felt: 2
trail: 1
patient: 1
dash: 2

BONUS ACTIVITY: A NOT–SO–SECRET MESSAGE!

Canada is the best!

SSR1146   ISBN: 9781771587327 © On The Mark Press